Overcoming Trauma

8 Steps to Healing the Past and Finding Peace Within

Allison Smiley

Overcoming Trauma: 8 Steps for Healing the Past

and Finding Peace Within

AllisonSmiley.com

Author photograph by Austin DuBois

ISBN 978-1-09832-999-0 (paperback)

ISBN 978-1-09833-000-2 (ebook)

Printed in the United States.

For my sweet daughter, Ava. I love you.

With Gratitude

My sincere gratitude and appreciation for everyone who helped make this book possible. To my editor, **Emma Moylan**, thank you for your skilled expertise and loving touch that went into these pages. To my ex-husband *Matt Smiley*, I'm grateful you are still my best friend and I appreciate everything you do for our family. Thanks for always believing in me, for the encouragement and support during this project. To *Ava Smiley*, my sweet child. Your bright light has been a beacon in the dark for me countless times over the years. Thank you for choosing me to be your momma.

To my Inner Alignment peeps – *Alicia LaGrone, Kodi Tujague, April Meullion, Jenn Jonas, Georgene Dvorak, Rebecca Robinette, Sara Madkour* – for holding such loving space for me to heal and learn what self-love truly means, and *Kim Beekman* for facilitating the healing of those deep core wounds. So much love and gratitude.

To my family – my parents, **Gary and Jackie Sandblom**, for the support, the opportunities for growth and healing, and the environment that made me strong and independent. My brother **Troy Sandblom**, for your IT wisdom and help, your sense of humor is a gift that I treasure. My uncle **Buzz Foster**, for your calm and wise guidance.

To **KimDiRe**, for your calming presence in my stormy weather, your believing eyes, your wisdom and higher awareness, and your light in those deep, dark moments when I couldn't find my way.

To my behind-the-scenes helpers – angels and archangels, my guides, angels, and higher self, and the Divine. Thanks for all the love, protection, wisdom, guidance, encouragement, and support, for always being there for me even when I thought I was all alone. I love you so much. Thank you.

Dragonfly Wisdom

A **note about the cover image:** The dragonfly symbolizes wisdom, transformation, and adaptability in life. Dragonflies remind us to bring more lightness and joy into our lives. They inspire us to bring about the changes needed for us to reach our full potential. The dragonfly has the ability to change direction quickly and glide through the air with ease. The wisdom of the dragonfly teaches us to be flexible and adaptable in any situation and encourages us to live and experience ourselves differently. When we open our hearts and our lives to the magic the dragonfly offers, we experience transformation and rebirth.

Table of Contents

Welcome

Welcome my lovely ones. I am so glad you have found *Overcoming Trauma: 8 Steps to Healing the Past and Finding Peace Within.* I have been teaching various parts of these steps for over a decade and have witnessed firsthand the amazing transformations that happen when they are practiced consistently.

I first created my trauma healing program, which includes all of my audio and video recordings, workbooks, and handouts, as well as group coaching and one-on-one sessions with me, as a way to personally guide people through the trauma healing process. Over the years, I have received requests for the information from former clients and others who were not able to go through the live program for whatever reason. So, in order to reach more people and continue my mission of helping those struggling to overcome the effects of trauma, I wrote this book and included the material that people receive when they go through my program personally with me. So let's begin.

Much love and blessings,

Allison

How to Download the Accompanying Material for the 8 Steps:

For each of the 8 steps, there are audio and video recordings, workbooks, and PDF handouts that you can download to use as you begin learning the steps and incorporating the daily practices into your routine. To access the material, visit www.overcomingtrauma.allisonsmiley.com. If you have any problem accessing the content, please contact ask@allisonsmiley.com.

Introduction

"Your vision will become clear only when you can look into your own heart.

Who looks outside, dreams; who looks inside, awakes." – Carl Jung

I first heard the word trauma in reference to myself was when I was attending a week-long intensive outpatient program in order to deal with yet another crisis of the mental breakdown variety. Over the years I had experienced many of these. These experiences were anywhere from what I call mini meltdowns where I was having panic attacks, anxiety, and chronic overwhelm to full-blown mental breakdowns that left me hospitalized with suicide attempts or voluntary hospitalizations knowing I was heading in that direction. Having your stomach pumped is an unpleasant experience and I'd learned over the years that although it felt like I was going to die, I didn't really want to die – I just wanted the pain to stop.

The intensive outpatient program I attended was one of those times when I had been hit hard by a life experience and didn't have any positive ways to cope with it. At the time, my fiancé had just called off our wedding after I told him about an abusive situation I had experienced when I was a young girl, and he felt that it was too much for our relationship to handle. He was angry that I hadn't told him sooner, and I was devastated by my worst fears coming true: his rejection of me because of my past trauma. I had only just started getting intense flashbacks and didn't know how to deal with what I was experiencing. I was also dealing with the humiliation and embarrassment from having to call off our wedding after finally getting engaged ten years into our relationship. My parents had rented a house in Mexico for the wedding ceremony, friends and relatives had bought plane tickets, and gifts had already started arriving at our home. My feelings vacillated from anger and rage at the betrayal to despair and depression as a result the self-loathing and shame I was experiencing. I spent several days curled up in a ball crying and wanting to die. So, the gifts went back to the store and I went to treatment.

I do want to mention here that he and I are very good friends and have an amicable co-parenting relationship with our daughter. Many years later I'm grateful for that moment in my life. If he hadn't had the courage to make the difficult decision to call things off, I may have never hit that bottom and had the opportunity to take a deep dive into my trauma issues. Intuitively he knew that we had both been significantly affected by trauma, and that we hadn't dealt with it yet. We didn't have the tools to handle the outer manifestations of our own inner demons much less navigate the tumultuous waters of our relationship. We were both self-medicating, he had been unfaithful to me with several women over the years, and neither of us could stay present for each other long enough to communicate effectively and build trust in order to make things work. We loved each other dearly, and truly wanted to spend the rest of our lives together, but it wasn't enough.

I learned about trauma for the first time during the intensive outpatient program I attended after the breakup. I felt both baffled and relieved at the same time to discover that trauma was the underlying issue. I was baffled because when I thought of trauma, I thought of soldiers returning from war, drive-by shootings, or natural disasters, and didn't see how I fit in with those folks. I was relieved because it finally made sense and things started falling into place like the missing pieces of a puzzle.

For over three decades, I had been trying to figure out what was wrong with me. I started reading self-help books when I was 12 years old. I went to a multitude of different therapists and therapy programs to address an array of issues I struggled with over the years – an eating disorder, overspending, depression, anxiety, OCD, relationship problems, impulsivity, suicidal ideation, and difficulty concentrating. Later, after years of living in such a high state of stress and anxiety (that I now understand to be called hypervigilance, a symptom of post-traumatic stress disorder or PTSD), my body began to break down and eventually fried out and I was diagnosed with multiple autoimmune issues including fibromyalgia and chronic fatigue.

It was like playing whack-a-mole, the game at the amusement park where toy moles take turns popping up out of holes and you try to hit them on the head with a mallet, but they pop up and down so fast that it's hard to get one. Or you do get one, but another pops up right after it, and another, and it's impossible to keep up with all the moles popping up and down. That's what dealing with the manifestations and symptoms of my trauma was like. I was focusing on one issue at a time and wasn't getting any relief at all, or when I'd start to feel the pain easing just a bit, another issue would pop up. It became so overwhelming, and I was frustrated at the lack of results and often felt hopeless and helpless. And angry, but mostly just angry with myself because I couldn't figure this thing out. I honestly felt like I had been dropped off on this planet by mistake and didn't know how to live in this world.

I didn't understand how people got up and went to work every day, came home to their families, went on vacations, and overall were basically happy. That wasn't my experience at all. Every day for as long as I could remember, it was a struggle to wake up and get through the day without wanting to die. I could get my life in order and keep it together for a little while, maybe a year or two, but eventually my inner world would catch up to my outer world and things would fall apart again. Over the years I had quit or been fired from more than 30 jobs, had moved more than 45 times and many of those moves were across the country, attempted suicide and had my stomach pumped twice, voluntarily hospitalized myself for suicidal thoughts twice, attended an intensive outpatient program, been to countless therapists, went on spiritual retreats, and studied with various well-known spiritual teachers. While these experiences have been invaluable and I've learned a lot from them, none of them eased my pain – at least not with any long-lasting results.

So I was delighted when I learned that all I had to do was get to the source of the trauma – the root cause of my pain – and heal it in order to end the whack-a-mole life I was living. I was in graduate school at the time and I was working toward a PhD in clinical psychology, so when I became aware of this concept of trauma and the healing of it, I switched my specialization from addiction to trauma and crisis response. I had been on this mission to figure out what was wrong with me and how I could fix it for almost three decades, and I read every book or blog I could find about trauma, including peer-reviewed articles and research studies on the subject. I thought if I just learned everything I could, then I could fix it and the pain would go away.

I was always in search of the next class, the next book, the next workshop, the next healing modality, or the next degree to get the answers I needed to finally experience some peace and relief from the emotional and physical pain. I tried just about everything – from spiritual studies to hypnotherapy and energy healing, to understanding how the brain and body respond to trauma, and eventually earning a master's degree in psychology with an emphasis on trauma and crisis. I studied with shamans, angel practitioners, energy healers, medical intuitives, new thought teachers, spiritual teachers, and holistic practitioners.

Prior to learning about trauma, I became certified in a number of healing modalities and felt called to help others, so I opened a private practice as a holistic practitioner and spiritual counselor. It was easier to focus on other people's problems than my own. For a number of years in my practice, I worked with clients and helped them overcome negative situations and habits, addictions, weight and body image issues, career and relationship issues. I was passionate about helping people get unstuck so they could move forward in their lives and pursue their goals and dreams. I also taught Reiki, meditation, and self-hypnosis at a local community college, and authored and recorded six guided meditation CDs and one on positive affirmations. I absolutely loved the work I was doing, but I was exhausted – physically, mentally, and emotionally – and I decided to close my practice. It was time to focus on me and address the trauma.

Over the next couple of years, I diligently went to trauma specialists who I thought could help me heal. The process felt excruciatingly slow, but I kept at it. Even when I wanted to quit or run, I stuck with it. I went to Al-Anon meetings and learned to set boundaries and techniques for self-care. I learned to tolerate discomfort and to sit calmly and stay present with pain in my body or with painful thoughts and emotions. I learned to let go of control and perfectionism, my false concepts of safety and security. I learned to slow down and to take care of my body and my mind. I learned to accept my present circumstances, whatever they may be. I learned that I could forgive myself and others who had harmed or betrayed me in some way. I learned that there was no next big cure, no miracle solution to my problems, and that there were no answers outside of myself. I learned that the only way through is through, that the courage to keep going is worth more than its weight in gold, and that I won't die from discomfort. But the most important thing I learned is that you *can* heal from trauma, even if you feel hopeless or helpless.

My goal in writing this book is to provide you with simple steps to help you overcome trauma and experience some peace in your life. When I started my journey to healing from trauma, I didn't have a road map to this process, and there was a lot of trial and error to find what worked and what didn't. I spent months focusing on techniques or healing methods that had little to no impact on overcoming and healing my trauma. I wish there had been an "Allison's Guide for Healing Her Trauma" program that I could have attended and that it had these 8 steps included in it.

Instead, I created that program myself, combining my master's degree in psychology where I received information on the latest neuroscience and techniques for healing trauma, with my holistic and spiritual training in clinical hypnotherapy, neurolinguistic programming (NLP), mindfulness and meditation, law of attraction principles, and various yogic practices. I started working with clients who began to see improvements in their symptoms almost immediately. I then offered an online trauma healing program where I guided people through the steps each week, provided weekly healing and group coaching sessions, as well as a private Facebook support group for trauma healing. The results have been amazing, and I wrote this book so that I could share the process with more people. The truth is, I used to believe that trauma healing was more about managing symptoms rather than truly being free of them, but I've experienced that freedom firsthand and it is delicious. I don't want anyone to suffer or struggle like I did, and I'm passionate about sharing this method for healing trauma so that you can experience that freedom too.

My hope for you is that you will use these steps to guide you to a calmer, more peaceful and joy-filled way of living. If you've been on this journey for a while like I have, you're probably worn out, ready to give up on ever feeling better, or are experiencing tremendous inner pain and turmoil. Your life may have become overwhelming or unbearable from living in a chronic high state of stress, trying to control everything around you, living with chronic physical pain or illness, or numbing the pain with substances or unhealthy behaviors. Hang in there and keep going because I know from experience that there is a way through it.

Thankfully, the topic of trauma has become more mainstream these days. There's less of a stigma around it and there are a lot more resources available for receiving help. If you're reading this book, then you've probably been informed about trauma in some way – whether it was mentioned by a therapist, brought up by a friend or family member, or you've been researching it on your own. Perhaps you know exactly what the problem is, but don't know how to deal with it or nothing so far has worked very well. Or perhaps this is all new to you and you don't know where to start. This book is written for all levels of trauma survivors, whether you are well versed in the concept or just dipping your toe in to see what it's about.

I've broken the book down into two sections: the first part provides a definition and the symptoms of trauma, the different types of trauma and survival responses, disorders that often occur with trauma, and how trauma affects the brain and body. I've also included chapters on toxic shame, perfectionism, and attachment because I've found these issues play a big role in the lives of trauma survivors. The first section gets a little science-y, but I feel that it's important to understand the connection between how trauma affects the mind, body, and spirit and how this disruption can have a devastating impact on people's lives.

The second section is where all the juicy material is and where healing can begin. It includes a chapter on building resilience – an important aspect of handling difficult situations and events in life. It also provides my proven method for overcoming trauma, which I've outlined in the 8 steps. Each step is then described in detail in its own chapter and exercises are provided to help you master each one. There is also a link to free material that you can access on my website that provides additional tools such as guided meditations, breathwork and yoga videos, and downloadable worksheets.

Take your time with each of the steps and work through them as thoroughly as possible. There is no need to rush, you are doing this for you. Be patient with yourself. Take your time. Sometimes you'll find that things might feel like they're getting worse before they get better. Just hang in there, go at a pace that feels right and trust me that it DOES get better and it is definitely worth it! If you're the kind of person who likes to read a book all the way through first, do that and then come back to the steps and spend some time working the exercises in each chapter. Some of the steps may come easily to you and may not take you much time, while others may be challenging and take you longer. You also might feel resistance to some of the steps and this is perfectly normal. Just remember … what you resist, persists. So, acknowledge your resistance but do the exercises anyway.

My experience has been that what I resist is where I *really* need the most healing at that time, and I've learned that if I avoid the issue then it will make itself known on a much grander scale until I deal with it. If you are really feeling a pushback, don't force it – you'll know when you're ready to work through it. There is no right or wrong way to working through these steps, so you can do one at a time or several at once. Do them in order or out of order. Whatever feels right to you.

I probably just sent all the perfectionists and rule followers running for the hills with that last statement – I know because I struggled with that too and preferred clear, concise instructions that I could execute easily, and yep, you guessed it, perfectly. Don't worry, we'll cover perfectionism and control in chapter 5.

Section I:

How Trauma Affect Us

Chapter 1

Trauma Overview

"Challenges are what make life interesting and overcoming them is what makes life meaningful." – Joshua J. Marine

About five years ago, I was in my psychiatrist's office for my monthly 15-minute appointment where I tell her how I am doing, and she writes me a prescription for medication. I no longer see a psychiatrist and I also don't take medications anymore for mental health, but at the time, it was what helped me get stable and to a place where I could begin to heal. I was telling her how I was learning dialectical behavioral therapy (DBT) to better regulate my emotions and improve distress tolerance. I found it to be very helpful, and my relationships with my friends and family and at work were improving as well. I told her I thought it really helped with managing my PTSD symptoms, and she replied in her thick, Eastern European accent, "I tink dat diagnosis is overused ... everyone dees day has PTSD!"

I admit I was a little shocked by her statement. I didn't take it personally, which I normally would have, so I noticed that I at least was making progress learning detachment. But still, her words surprised me because I had assumed that all practitioners in the mental health field understood trauma and the devastating symptoms and life challenges that people struggling with it face every day. Is it a bad thing that more people are being diagnosed with PTSD now than ever before? I feel that this trend will continue as trauma awareness increases and more and more resources for healing become available.

The topic of PTSD was mostly ignored until the 1970s at the end of the Vietnam War and the diagnosis was included in the *DSM-III* (*Diagnostic Statistical Manual* is what licensed professionals use to determine mental health diagnoses) to explain the veterans' etiological symptoms. PTSD is no longer reserved solely for combat veterans as anyone who meets diagnostic criteria can be a candidate for this disorder: individuals such as survivors of natural disasters or school shootings, victims of violent assault or domestic abuse, and adult survivors of childhood abuse. It's not like someone wakes up one day and says, "Boy, I'd like to struggle with symptoms of PTSD and I hope I get diagnosed with it!" No, the reason the diagnosis numbers are rising is because of increased awareness and training on the signs and symptoms among doctors and practitioners. Research on trauma and the effects it has on the mind, body, and spirit continues to grow and shed light on this previously under-acknowledged category of psychology and medicine.

It is now known and generally recognized that there are two types of PTSD: standard PTSD and complex PTSD. In recent years, the concept of complex PTSD came about because many doctors and mental health practitioners noticed that there are individuals with trauma psychopathology that do not fit into the standard PTSD diagnostic criteria. Judith Hermann first posited the question in 1991 of whether complex PTSD should be recognized as its own separate and distinct disorder in the *DSM-IV*. In her clinical work with individuals who had experienced prolonged exposure to trauma, she noticed a distinct set of symptoms that were different from standard PTSD symptoms.

She proposed that a separate diagnosis of complex PTSD be created and published in the *DSM-IV*. I wrote my master's thesis on this topic, which I find fascinating, but I won't bore you with the details of it all. To summarize, the proposal was denied, but there are now psychologists and doctors who have dedicated their careers to studying complex PTSD and are developing effective treatments to address its unique symptomology. Some of these techniques such as dialectical behavioral therapy (DBT) and mindfulness-based practices are incorporated into the steps I outline in section two.

Defining PTSD and Complex PTSD

The American Psychiatric Association (APA) defines post-traumatic stress disorder as a psychological disorder that happens when an individual experiences a traumatic event, such as a school shooting or natural disaster. The APA includes a list of diagnostic criteria that the individual needs to meet in order to be identified as having PTSD. In addition to experiencing a traumatic event, the criteria includes four clusters of symptoms that the individual must be experiencing. Those clusters of symptoms are intrusion, avoidance, negative alterations in cognition and mood, and alterations in arousal and reactivity. I'll go into these symptoms in more detail shortly.

Complex PTSD is defined by the Medical Dictionary as a "psychological state induced by prolonged psychosocial trauma coupled with disempowerment and an inability to escape one's situation." Examples of prolonged exposure to trauma are sexual abuse, physical abuse, emotional abuse, torture, and domestic violence. Although complex PTSD is similar to PTSD, PTSD does not account for all of the symptoms of complex PTSD and doesn't take into account the inescapability and helplessness that characterizes complex PTSD. Complex PTSD has also been referred to as "disorders of extreme stress not otherwise specified" (DESNOS) to describe the cluster of symptoms that are not included in the PTSD diagnostic criteria in the *DSM-V*.

Types of Trauma

I believe that there are three categories of trauma – PTSD, complex PTSD, and vicarious trauma. Not all trauma experts currently agree on separating standard PTSD and complex PTSD. One thing that is becoming apparent with the new information emerging on trauma, however, is that there are two different types of trauma – a single trauma and chronic trauma – that affect individuals differently. A recent study by Cloitre showed that single traumas are more predictive of an individual developing PTSD, compared to long-term or chronic trauma that is more predictive of complex PTSD. The results of this study were the impetus for the recommendation of the World Health Organization International Classification of Diseases, 11th version (ICD-11) to include two classifications of PTSD: one for standard PTSD and one for complex PTSD.

As mentioned earlier, long-term exposure to trauma is predictive of the development of complex PTSD. Studies show that physical and sexual abuse as well as severe neglect in childhood are more likely to cause PTSD than other types of trauma. The percentage of individuals who develop PTSD due to trauma is typically around 8–20 percent compared to 50 percent for those who develop PTSD due to childhood abuse and neglect. Moreover, these individuals are more likely to develop complex PTSD, which can also include personality disorders and are more difficult to treat with standard PTSD treatment.

The third type of trauma is vicarious trauma. It's not one that you read or hear about often unless you're a mental health practitioner or emergency responder. Because these professionals are exposed to clients who have experienced trauma or they are on-site responding to victims of natural disasters, shootings, or other crises, they are exposed to trauma through the people they are helping. So, while they didn't experience the trauma directly, they are reliving it with their client in their office or they are witnessing the devastation after the fact. This type of exposure can create symptoms in individuals that mimic PTSD, even though they weren't the victim. These professionals are usually trained in setting boundaries, avoiding burnout, and not taking on their clients' stuff. However, we're all human and sometimes we can get affected by vicarious trauma or secondary trauma as it's also known. I've worked with so many sensitive people and other healing professionals, and I believe that it's entirely possible to inadvertently take on other people's traumas without realizing it. Even though this isn't quite as well known as our traditional thoughts on what trauma is, I want to bring it to your awareness in case you or a loved one might be experiencing this type of trauma.

Symptoms of Standard PTSD

Most people experience stress after a traumatic event, and this is a normal reaction. Symptoms of PTSD typically last longer than three months after the traumatic event, but it can sometimes take years for them to appear in the individual's life. PTSD symptoms are often very disruptive and can have a negative impact on a person's work, school, or home life. Living with symptoms of PTSD on a daily basis can be very challenging for most people and it's often a struggle for them to just get through the day.

There are four categories of symptoms for standard PTSD: intrusive memories, avoidance, changes in emotional reaction, and negative changes in thinking or mood. *Intrusive memories* is having nightmares about the event, experiencing flashbacks – which are the reliving of the event as if it were happening in the present time – and recurring unwanted memories of the event that are distressing. *Avoidance* is attempting to avoid thinking or talking about the event or avoiding people or places that trigger memories of the event. *Changes in emotional reactions* are also referred to as hyperarousal or hypervigilance. This is when the body is stuck in the flight mode of the fight or flight response to danger. I will discuss more about this in chapter 3 on how trauma affects the body. When this happens, an individual exists constantly in an anxious, high-stress state and is

23

prone to irritability and angry outbursts, has difficulty concentrating, has difficulty falling asleep or staying asleep, startles easily, and is always on guard. *Negative changes in thinking or mood* can present in individuals as feeling numb, not being able to have positive thoughts, having negative feelings about themselves or others, lack of interest in activities they once enjoyed, and feelings of hopelessness.

Symptoms of Complex PTSD

There are three main symptoms that practitioners and researchers agree are signs of complex PTSD. These symptoms for complex PTSD are different from, but in addition to, all of the symptoms for standard PTSD. They are called somatization, dissociation, and affect dysregulation. *Somatization* is the experience of chronic physical problems or unexplained chronic pain that many trauma survivors experience. *Dissociation* is a safety mechanism in the brain that allows the individual to separate from the trauma or triggers to be able to function in everyday life. *Affect dysregulation* is the inability to effectively manage emotions from triggers, as well as impulse controls, inaccurate self-perception and perception of others, and skewed systems of meaning.

Because of the multitude of symptoms that individuals with complex PTSD present with, they are often underdiagnosed or misdiagnosed resulting in ineffective treatment. Even worse, they may be improperly diagnosed with bipolar, narcissistic, or borderline personality disorders and seen as having character defects that can't be overcome. Even OCD and ADHD have been considered as nothing more than stress responses to PTSD triggers, rather than separate disorders. This can bring about more shame and hopelessness for someone who is already living an emotional nightmare.

You may recognize many or all of these symptoms in yourself or a loved one, which could mean they are more than likely struggling with PTSD in one form or another. People can live for years suffering from the symptoms and effects of PTSD and not even know they have it or what is going on with them. This was my experience – I struggled day after day, year after year with it and pretty much white-knuckled my way through life trying to keep it together. The more awareness people have about PTSD, the more that people will seek help. Over 30 percent of individuals experiencing symptoms of PTSD go undiagnosed each year. No one knows exactly why this is, but it is most likely due to a lack of awareness, lack of resources available for treatment, as well as the fear of the stigma attached to a mental health diagnosis. This is one of the main reasons I wrote this book. No one should have to live with untreated PTSD, not even for a day.

Big Ts and Little ts

One thing that tripped me up when I first started learning about trauma and then deciding to begin the process of healing it, was that it was hard for me to feel that I had qualifying trauma compared to those who had witnessed the ravages of war, experienced the devastation of a natural disaster, or who were injured in a terrible accident. However, when I began processing through my experiences with a trauma specialist, it became clear that I had experienced not just major traumas in my life, but multiple smaller traumas as well.

Trauma experts like to describe trauma in terms of big "Ts" and little "ts." Big Ts would be considered as childhood abuse or neglect, domestic violence or a violent attack such as rape or mugging, being in combat, loss of a loved one, or being in a serious automobile accident. Little ts would be described as changing jobs or moving, disagreements with loved ones, a traffic ticket, being criticized by a boss, a minor injury, or a breakup of a relationship – although this could be considered a big T depending on the relationship. The important thing to understand about trauma is that no one other than you can tell you if you were traumatized or not. And only you know if it was a big T or little t, because everyone has their experiences from their own perspectives. No one could possibly know how you felt, what you thought, or what your pain level was in that moment.

No trauma is too big or too small. It doesn't matter the size of the trauma, it's the impact that it had on the individual that matters. Trauma is highly individualized, since a trauma experienced by one person might not be a big deal, but another person might be devastated by it. Individuals can develop PTSD without ever experiencing what would be considered a major trauma. They can have many smaller traumas that eventually add up and they hit their breaking point. Other lesser-known situations such as psychological or emotional abuse, chronic illness, losses of varying kinds, emotional neglect, and religious, cultural, or social trauma can cause the onset of PTSD.

Only you can decide what is a big T or little t to you, and don't let anyone ever shame you into thinking otherwise. I had a client, who when talking about her issues, would shrug her shoulders and say something like, "Well, I grew up in the back of a liquor store, so this isn't really a big deal." She would always minimize her current situation and not allow herself to feel what was going on in the present moment. When I asked her about it, she said that she learned to early on as a result of a family member who constantly shamed her whenever she complained about things. As a result, she developed a strategy of pushing aside or downplaying big issues or events that were really affecting her.

The Four Fs

In his book *Complex PTSD: From Surviving to Thriving*, Pete Walker describes what he calls the Four Fs, which are four types of survival responses. Most people have heard of the fight and flight responses to danger, where the central nervous system kicks in and gives the individual the ability to react to the situation. Walker identifies four, rather than two, responses to danger and that over time individuals tend to rely on one type as their survival response when triggered. These four responses are fight, flight, fawn, and freeze. Different environmental factors such as the type of trauma experienced, birth order, and genetic predisposition can influence how an individual will develop their type of response.

Additionally, the four types can also be identified with different disorders or personality types, which make it easier to understand how a misdiagnosis can happen. As with any maladaptive patterns and defenses, they are initially used as protection and a means of surviving in an abusive or neglectful household. Later in life, however, these defenses become very restrictive for the individual and can create a challenging and unmanageable reaction to life's stresses.

Fight: First, let's describe the fight response (this type tends to exhibit more of a narcissistic personality or behavior) – it's an aggressive response that is triggered by a perceived threat. It can manifest in ways such as bullying, picking fights verbally or physically, raging, aggressive driving, or degrading others. This type has a belief that power and control can create a feeling of safety, secure love, and prevent painful feelings of abandonment. I like to think of this response as being similar to a lion with a thorn in its paw. He can be mean and dangerous if he feels threatened, but underneath he's really just hurting and needs some nurturing.

Flight: Next is the flight response (this type is more of an obsessive/compulsive personality or behavior) – it's a fleeing response such as walking out of a perceived threatening situation, moving, breaking up a relationship or friendship, or changing jobs. It can also be demonstrated in not just a physical fleeing but fleeing by going into overdrive or a hyperactive state and can manifest as going nonstop, focusing only on getting things done, to-do lists, running errands, never-ending projects, and can often take place in a frantic way with lack of direction. This type has an unconscious belief that perfection will make them safe and loveable. They are also susceptible to stimulant addiction and addiction to their own adrenaline as well as process addictions such as busyness. This type was my personal go-to trauma response and I still occasionally need to keep an eye on myself with this. When I start placing too much importance on getting things done or taking on too much and overtaxing myself – this is a sure sign for me to slow down and ground myself and try to get to the root of what is causing me to feel unsafe and resolve it.

Freeze: The next type is the freeze response (this one is more of a dissociative personality or behavior) – this response is like a numbing out, checking out mentally, realizing that resisting is futile and could potentially cause harm. This trauma response would be demonstrated in Netflix binges, computer gaming, and lying down or sleeping a lot. There is a belief here that safety is found in solitude. Where the flight type is stuck in the "on" position, the freeze type can be perceived as stuck in the "off" position. Walker describes this type as usually the most profoundly abandoned child. Freeze types often dissociate, daydream, and disconnect. They are prone to opioid or sedating substance addictions and avoid social situations due to the fear of feeling abandonment pain.

Fawn: Finally, there is the fawn response (this type would be like a codependent personality or behavior) – this is a response that consists of trying to please others or finding ways to be helpful in order to avoid harm or attack. This trauma response type typically takes on the needs and wants of others and doesn't have a clear idea of their own, having given them up early in life to keep peace or avoid attack. There is a belief that they have to give up their own needs, rights, and boundaries in order to experience love and safety. They are usually the child of a narcissistic parent and were often shamed or scared out of developing a healthy sense of ego. *Healthy Sense of ego?*

So those are the four Fs, the four types of responses to trauma. If you don't identify with any of them or if you identify with more than one, don't worry – most people are usually hybrids of the four Fs, although you might lean toward one type more predominantly. Also, none of these types are bad and can actually be healthy and helpful when accessed appropriately in response to real danger. Just like we understand that the "fight or flight" response to danger is helpful when facing a bear in the woods, these types can assist us in navigating an appropriate response to a real threat. It's only when a traumatized individual learns to survive by over-relying on the use of one or two of the four types of responses. It then becomes limiting and keeps the individual stuck in unresolved trauma.

Chapter 2

The Brain and Trauma

"The brain is a wonderful organ; it starts working the moment you get up in the morning and does not stop until you get into the office." – Robert Frost

"Are you able to hear what I'm saying?" My boyfriend years ago often asked this during our frequent difficult discussions that we had while we were together. He'd learned to ask me this after one particularly long phone conversation where he spent two hours convincing me of something, and I hadn't heard a word he said. I just kept going back to the original comment that triggered me and hadn't been able to take in or process anything he said after that. I heard the words he was saying, they just weren't registering in my brain and I wasn't able to respond to anything new he was saying.

I later learned that trauma can have a significant impact on the brain. While much of the brain develops while in utero, it continues to develop after a person is born. Children develop both white and grey matter up to about five years of age. From seven to seventeen years after birth, usually only grey matter develops. Traumatic stress can create lasting changes in certain brain areas and is related to acute and chronic changes in neurochemical systems such as dysregulation of norepinephrine and cortisol, which are released in response to stress. Long-term dysregulation of norepinephrine and cortisol affects the HPA axis (hippocampus, prefrontal cortex, and the amygdala), which is how the response to stress is regulated. The three major players in the brain that are affected by trauma are the hippocampus, prefrontal cortex, and the amygdala.

Hippocampus: The hippocampus plays an important role in memory and emotion regulation. It is responsible for recalling memory and differentiating between past and present experiences. An increase in the stress hormone glucocorticoid kills cells in the hippocampus, causing it to become less effective in being able to make synaptic connections that are required for memory consolidation. The hippocampus doesn't receive the message that the threat is in the past and in response sends a message that there is a threat present.

The hippocampus also loses volume and decreases in size due to elevated stress hormones, which can cause gaps in memory

34

of everyday events as well as in verbal memory. In children with a history of trauma such as abuse or neglect, the hippocampus fails to develop properly. Because of the smaller volume of grey matter due to underdevelopment, the brain overcompensates by having the neurotransmitters receive a bigger "hit" than normal when processing emotions. This means that individuals with smaller hippocampi tend to feel things more intensely, deeply, and for a longer period of time, which is believed to contribute to their challenges with emotion regulation. It also takes these individuals longer to return to a normal baseline state after experiencing such intense emotion.

The Amygdala: The amygdala is a small, almond-shaped part of the brain that is located deep in the middle of the temporal lobe. It stores emotional or threat-related memories and is responsible for emotional memory and fear responses, detecting threats in the environment, and activating the fight or flight response. The amygdala activates the sympathetic nervous system to handle the threat or danger. Individuals with trauma history tend to have an enlarged and overactive amygdala, which is continuously sending the stress response message to release more epinephrine and cortisol, causing the individual to experience hyperarousal, hypervigilance, and sleep disturbance.

A hyperactive amygdala communicates with the insula, a part of the brain that is associated with introspection, emotional awareness, and reactions to sensory information. Because the amygdala mainly stores emotional memories and fear responses, the message it sends to the insula can cause a plethora of negative emotions and few positive emotions. Positive memories have a beginning, middle, and end. Traumatic memories are fragmented, disorganized, filled with gaps, and manifest as images, sensations, and intense emotions. Having a reactive amygdala causes impulsivity because it is not being properly regulated by the prefrontal cortex. Individuals have less control over reactive anger and impulsive behaviors when emotionally triggered, causing irreparable damage to careers and relationships.

Prefrontal Cortex: The prefrontal cortex regulates attention and awareness and makes decisions about the best response to a situation. It is responsible for initiating conscious, voluntary behavior and determines the meaning and emotional significance of events. It is supposed to regulate emotions and inhibit or correct any type of dysfunctional reaction, calming down the flight or fight response if it isn't needed at that time. The prefrontal cortex is smaller in volume and has decreased function in individuals with PTSD, so it is less activated and doesn't regulate the threat response.

Unfortunately, this allows the amygdala to run the show from its overactive state and the body is unable to regulate the consistently elevated stress hormones, causing the sympathetic nervous system to stay highly active and leading to fatigue, especially in the adrenals.

Going back to the situation at the beginning of the chapter where I couldn't hear and process the conversation after being triggered, you can probably see the areas of the brain that had affected me at that time. First, there was a comment made that my hippocampus couldn't differentiate between a threat from the past and the present moment. Then, the amygdala tapped into stored emotional memories and fear responses and sent out the signals to activate my sympathetic nervous system and send my body into fight or flight. This in turn resulted in shutting down my prefrontal cortex and any ability I had in that moment to create a logical, conscious thought and respond to the comment.

Although it seems a little overwhelming to think about these different areas of the brain running amok due to trauma and stress responses, we now know that the brain has plasticity and is capable of rewiring itself and learning new ways of doing things. The amygdala can learn to chill out, the hippocampus can learn to differentiate between past and present, and the prefrontal cortex can learn to regulate decision-making and impulsivity. And the sympathetic nervous system can learn to return to a relaxed state, giving the adrenals a much-needed break. The tools that are presented in the 8 steps in section two will help you work with your brain in developing these new skills.

Chapter 3

The Body and Trauma

"The body is a self-healing organism, so it's really about clearing things out of the way so the body can heal itself." – Barbara Brennan

About nine years ago, I was out to dinner with friends and two guys were sitting at a table nearby. They were talking very loudly and having a heated discussion about something. I had taken a bite of food but I couldn't taste anything, and I had a hard time swallowing the food down. My heart was racing, and I felt hot, lightheaded and dizzy, nauseous, and I was shaking and sweating profusely. I looked around the table at my friends and no one even seemed to notice the guys talking or that anything was amiss. All I knew was that I *had* to get out of there. I handed one of my friends some money and told her I'd meet her outside. After sitting on a bench outside the restaurant in relative quiet for about 20 minutes, my body and nerves finally returned to a relatively normal state. I had no idea what just happened, but I knew it probably wasn't good. Years later I now understand that I was having a somatic flashback and my body was responding by sending messages that I needed to get to safety right away.

The body is an incredibly intelligent, living organism and has the innate ability to heal and regulate itself. When an individual experiences traumatic stress and it is not properly processed, the systems in the body go haywire and it gets reset into believing that the world is a dangerous and terrifying place and it feels unsafe to live in. Unresolved trauma that is stored in the body can later manifest as health problems and mental illness. Studies have linked health problems, obesity, and mental health issues to adverse childhood experiences (ACEs), and the higher number of ACEs you experienced, the higher the chance is that you'll be affected by these medical and mental health issues. Here's a link that you can use to take the ACE's quiz and find out your score.

This was a groundbreaking discovery and brought awareness to the ongoing health crisis our country is currently experiencing from the medical and mental health issues that have resulted from unresolved childhood trauma. The list of the lasting effects of traumatic stress is a long one – it can predispose us to everything from diabetes to heart disease, and have an impact on employment, education, families, relationships, crime rates, and can lead to abusive or addictive behaviors and habits. The consequences of unresolved childhood trauma have taken the lives of more Americans than both the Iraq and Afghanistan wars combined since 2001, and the serious health issues that arise from trauma are twice as likely to affect women in the United States than breast cancer.

As discussed earlier in the brain section, traumatic stress in childhood such as abuse and neglect, impact the developing brain. Self-regulation is learned from the child's parents or caretakers and is often inadequate. Studies have shown that drugs and conventional talk therapy are not able to rectify the changes made to the brain's wiring from early trauma exposure. Bessel Van der Kolk, a leading trauma specialist, realized the devastating impact that adverse childhood experiences had – particularly with the loss of identity, feelings of being trapped, frozen and powerless, and the traumatic imprint on the brain – and the way in which the whole world seems filled with triggers for abused children. He proposed that a diagnosis of child development trauma be added in the *DSM-V* in 2013, and although the request was denied, he continues to provide the latest research and treatment techniques for those suffering from the effects of trauma.

Now that you understand the connection between unresolved trauma and health and mental health issues, let's go into more about how trauma affects the body in the first place. Our body is constantly communicating through electrical and chemical impulses, sending messages informing our body on what to do. It filters what it needs to pay attention to and what doesn't need attention and prioritizes it. This is how it runs under normal conditions, but under stress this all goes out the window.

When we process memories, they get categorized as explicit or implicit. Explicit memories consist of factual data and autobiographical information. Implicit memories are connected to feeling, emotional responses, and sensations in the body. These memories travel along different pathways in the brain and are later formed into an integrated memory. Under traumatic stress, chemical messengers are streaming through the blood system telling you to run, and their primary job is getting you away to safety. This is one of the main reasons that individuals who have experienced trauma have gaps in their memory. The body shuts everything down in order to get to safety.

As I touched on briefly in the brain part, the body has a sympathetic and parasympathetic nervous system. The parasympathetic nervous system is also known as the rest and digest system. It slows the heart rate down, conserves energy, and increases intestinal and gland activity. The sympathetic nervous system activates in times of danger and high stress, releasing the stress hormones cortisol and norepinephrine to counter pain, and adrenaline runs through the body as fuel for energy. Blood pressure increases, breath rate increases to pull in oxygen for the muscles, there's an increase in endorphins, and blood is diverted from the extremities. The body shuts down other functioning areas during the stress response such as hunger, digestion, and the urge to use the bathroom. This is all in the immediate preparation for an attack or escape.

This is all a normal and helpful situation when presented with a real threat of danger. However, when an individual undergoes repeated periods of stress, such as with ongoing trauma, they get stuck. The amygdala becomes very sensitive and overreactive. The brain quits processing and only focuses on keeping you safe and away from danger. The memories don't get fully processed and are stored in fragmented parts as implicit and explicit memories. This explains why certain smells, touch, or tone of voice can be triggers for individuals with PTSD.

The body can't tell the difference between emotional and physical danger. It processes the message of physical symptoms = physical danger = run like hell. Many of the body's organs require the parasympathetic and sympathetic nervous systems to work together in balance. When the body is in overdrive from a chronic state of stress hormones flooding it, physical illness, chronic pain, and autoimmune issues can result. I've found that traumatized individuals often sever the relationship with their bodies and are disconnected from them. They usually do this by dissociating and by numbing themselves with drugs, alcohol, or food, or they completely shut down their emotional awareness.

Through these processes, trauma gets stuck in the body. Animals who survive an attack can just get up, physically shake it off, and run away. This is difficult for humans to do because the threat isn't always obvious, or it's chronic and lasts longer like abuse and neglect. I remember thinking about this concept a few years ago and noticed how my dog Stella got into a skirmish with another dog, shook it off, and then continued on her walk. I wondered why I couldn't do this, and when I asked my therapist about it, she said, "Well, your dog wasn't held down and trapped, fearing for its life and unable to escape the danger." OK, fair point. We are all in a different place in the healing journey, so comparing myself to anyone, including my dog, was probably unhelpful anyway.

The body remembers everything – sounds, smells, touches, tastes – even if we have no memory of those things. Our cells store memories and information about our experiences, even if we aren't always consciously aware of them. The experiences could have happened when we were too young to remember, or we might have blocked them out. I know some people who barely remember their childhood, and others who have a hard time forgetting it. The trauma is experienced at the emotional level and then stored at the cellular level, so even if we don't remember what happened, our bodies have stored it away for recall and processing later.

Body memories are often the last to be addressed and can sometimes take longer to be healed. Memories, flashbacks, pain, or illness are the body's way of getting your attention. It's asking you to pay attention and telling you that it's time to heal. Living in a chronic state of stress and hypervigilance took a toll on my body. I had three different autoimmune issues I was dealing with along with chronic pain in my left shoulder and knee. I spent years working on healing my trauma, processing memories, and calming down my nervous system. But I still reacted to sensory triggers like loud noises, tone of voice, or physical touch. It didn't matter how much I knew or understood about trauma, it was useless when my body was still holding on to it.

When I finally began feeling the emotions, processing them, and letting them go, my body began to heal. I was stabilized enough that connecting with my body didn't trigger me like it used to. I could notice the pain or discomfort I was feeling, and then I allowed any memories to come up so I could acknowledge them and release them. As I went through this process over a period of months, every so often a bruise in the shape of a thumb or hand would appear on my arms or thighs. At first it was a little freaky and I thought maybe I should be the star of the next paranormal movie, but I learned that this phenomenon was called somatic bruising and that it was a way that the body releases the stored trauma and memories.

It's critical to allow the body the time and space to heal from trauma, not only because of the importance of freeing yourself from reliving the trauma again and again, but also because of the devastating medical and mental health issues holding on to trauma long term can cause. There are some great modalities out there for releasing trauma from the body, and we're going to incorporate some of them in the steps to overcoming trauma in section two. Yoga, qigong, somatic experiencing (SE), body talk, Rolfing, and cranial sacral therapy are all ways to use mindful movement to release trauma from the body. I've also included some information and links in the additional resources section.

Chapter 4

Toxic Shame

"If we share our story with someone who responds with empathy and understanding, shame can't survive." — Brené Brown

I used to think that everything was my fault. And I mean everything. My grandfather had a heart attack and died when I was in sixth grade, and we had just visited him the month before. He had a boat on Lake Powell, and he taught me how to water ski. He was so proud of how quickly I learned to get up on those skis and we took quite a few turns around the lake. When I saw him lying in the casket at his funeral, I began sobbing uncontrollably. I hadn't cried at all up until that point, but when I saw him, I just knew that I had killed him. I thought if I had caught on more quickly, if I hadn't fallen down so much, or if I hadn't stayed up so long during my turn on those skis, maybe he'd still be alive. The truth was that he was 57 years old, overweight, lived a high-stress lifestyle, smoked and drank heavily, and ate mostly red meat and potatoes. A heart attack killed him, not me. But when you live with toxic shame, everything is your fault.

Shame is normally a healthy, human emotion. It keeps us in humility and reminds us that we're going to make mistakes, and it helps us learn from them. In its healthy form, shame directs us back on the path of mindfulness and reminds us of our limits. Shame is something we feel, acknowledge, adjust from, and move on from. It allows us to get in touch with our core needs when we are dependent on others, and it helps us understand that we need to love and be in loving relationships with others.

Toxic shame, on the other hand, tells us that we didn't *do* something bad but that we *are* something bad. It takes us to the very depths of our beliefs of unworthiness, and says that we are not good enough and are inherently flawed and defective as a human being. Toxic shame is so devastating to individuals because they are afraid of exposing their true selves to anyone, even themselves. So they end up creating a false self, and when they create the false self, they lose their identity and connection to life, living in emptiness and the devastation of abandonment.

When a child is raised in an extremely rejecting and critical family, she takes on the belief that even her basic needs and feelings are inherent imperfections, and that any ill-treatment of her is justified. Just the act of asking for lunch money or a ride to school can cause extreme panic, and spiral into fear of rejection and abandonment. However, the child somehow always holds out hope that the parent will someday approve of her, and she continues to strive for that approval by achieving more, doing better, or being the best. It's a thankless goal though, and usually leaves the child feeling more rejected and abandoned than ever. This just creates a perpetuating cycle of perfectionism and a false sense of worthiness by doing. Once the child realizes that her accomplishments will never attain the goal of the much-desired parental approval, the foundation she's built for herself in order to create a sense of safety and love, will collapse. This may not happen until years later, but it continues to fan the flames of self-loathing and toxic shame.

Toxic shame is usually multi-generational and passed down through families. It comes with the desire to keep secrets hidden, and that only the positive things are shown to the outside world. Secrets such as alcoholism, abuse, neglect, incest, mental illness, money problems, and addictions are hidden within the family, and perpetuate the cycle of toxic shame because they are never addressed and healed. There are rules that must be followed in the family such as not talking about the secrets, always being in control, blaming others or self when things go wrong, not making mistakes, and not trusting others. Other unspoken rules are that the parents are in charge, to protect the parents at all costs, that the kids will must be broken, the child is responsible for the parents' anger, and the child's needs and feelings are a threat to the parents. If the rules are broken, serious punishments are handed down, or worse, the child may be disowned or kicked out of the family.

Internalized shame becomes toxic shame. When a child is abandoned, whether physically or emotionally, by neglect or abuse, or they are highly rejected and criticized by family members, they experience the loss of self and a deep-seated depression takes place. John Bradshaw calls this the "hole in your soul phenomena," and it leaves the person with a sense of emptiness and a feeling that life is meaningless. All types of abuse are recognized as abandonment, and the abuse/abandonment provides the setting for internalizing shame. Once shame is internalized, it becomes the ruler of all the other emotions. Shame trumps everything and binds the other emotions to it. Fear to express emotions emerges since that would expose shame, and repressed emotions become too big and overwhelming. Parents who are shame-bound can't allow their children to express emotions, otherwise it will trigger their own emotions and shame.

To live with toxic shame is to exist in excruciating emotional pain. Physical pain can be unbearable at times, but it usually comes and goes. The emotional pain of toxic shame is never-ending because of the belief that you are inherently defective. It's hopeless and can't be fixed. To manage the excruciating emotional pain, most people will turn to mood-altering substances to provide that much-needed defense against the empty abyss of shame. Using substances such as drugs, alcohol or food provides relief from the pain of shame, but it also becomes a necessity, and addiction often forms. It becomes a cycle of the shame feeding the addiction and addiction feeding the shame.

For years when I woke up triggered and full of self-loathing, my knee-jerk reaction was to restrict my food and pound my body into the ground with a long run or hard workout. I didn't know anything about shame or triggers at the time, but it was most likely my need for control over the emotional pain as well as some underlying desire to please my family by "eating right and looking good" that drove this pattern. When an individual experiences self-hatred or self-loathing, it's because they can't get angry at the person (or people) they're supposed to be angry with and they turn the emotion inward. They also don't have compassion for their inner child and have a belief that they were a difficult child or deserved the abuse.

That's the thing about toxic shame, it's insidious and runs to the core of the being, so it can be a challenge to bring about awareness for the need to liberate the true self from the shackles of shame. One thing that helps is to begin grieving childhood losses and allowing room for self-compassion to emerge. There is no room for toxic shame when grief and compassion are present. Another thing to do is make a commitment to show up for yourself. Because toxic shame is based in abandonment, showing up for yourself no matter what, sends the shame packing. I had a difficult time showing up for appointments or pretty much any commitments I'd made. It was hard pulling myself out of isolation and summoning up the energy to go anywhere, even for things that were good for me or that I really needed, like therapy appointments or massages.

After decades of feeling like I wasn't important and my needs and feelings weren't important, it took some determination to convince myself otherwise. But once I'd made that commitment and began showing up again and again, I got better at it and found that I really enjoyed it too. One thing that I found happening when I first started was that I couldn't take care of myself when I was triggered. All bets were off, and everything went out the window. So, I changed my commitment to myself that I would show up and take care of my needs, *especially* when I was triggered. That made all the difference, and now it's not even a thing I have to think about, I just do it.

The final thing I recommend for dealing with toxic shame is to begin challenging the thoughts you have about yourself. Most likely, the thought patterns and loops playing in your mind aren't even yours to begin with. When you think something negative about yourself, start asking yourself these three things: Is it necessary? Is it kind? Is it true? Now your toxic shame will probably say, "Yes, it's true!" But … is it really? Some people like to name their negative inner voice and talk back to it. They'll say in their heads, "Not today, Betty, I'm keeping things positive in here" or whatever feels right at that time. I also like Louise Hay's technique where she'd say to her negative voice, "Thank you for sharing" and then follow it up with something positive. It doesn't matter which approach you use, do whatever works for you. Once you begin to really challenge that negative inner talk, things will begin to shift and toxic shame can then become a distant memory.

Chapter 5

Perfectionism

"Perfectionism is the voice of the oppressor, the enemy of the people. It will keep you cramped and insane your whole life." – Anne Lamott

It was go time. My course was ready to launch after months of recording audios and videos, creating worksheets, guided meditations, positive affirmations, and even some cute memes and infographics. But I couldn't pull the trigger and put it out there. I kept going back in and tweaking things, rearranging the modules, and adding another recording or video. I was stalling because I wasn't ready to launch it. Why? Because it didn't feel like it was good enough, perfect enough, or maybe it was too much. I wondered if it would help people, if they would want their money back, if it would be a total flop. Normally, I completely trusted in the Divine whenever I teach a class, produce a CD, or work with clients. I know without a doubt that I'm just a conduit for the information or healing coming through, so I don't question it, and allow it to flow. Why was this time so different? Maybe because this wasn't just some Reiki or meditation class, or psychic development workshop. This course was about trauma, an in-your-face, up-close, and personal topic for me, and I felt vulnerable and exposed.

Perfectionism, like toxic shame, has its roots in the fear of rejection, abandonment, and unworthiness. Shame arises from the fear of being unlovable, and feelings of unworthiness provide the diet for the insatiable hunger of perfectionism. Being a perfectionist is like having the meanest, cruelest person you know by your side at all times, judging and criticizing you, and making condescending remarks about everything you do. Yet despite that, you still hold out hope that if you can just do things right, that person will love you and accept you. It is a never-ending cycle of unhappiness because there is never enough to accomplish, achieve, or perfect, so it's never done and it's never good enough. No matter how good it is, it is not enough.

Most perfectionists had narcissistic or perfectionistic parents. Children of perfectionists and narcissists learn to adapt to their highly critical, rejecting, and invalidating environment by believing that if they just do better, achieve more, and be the best, they will be loved and accepted. They become obsessed with achieving, only focused on attaining the next goal, and are reluctant to delegate tasks or let go of control for fear of it not being done the "right way." They are always future-focused, never able to accept the way things are in the present moment, and unable to enjoy the process or journey to the goal, and they become stuck in a perpetual loop of never-ending dissatisfaction and unhappiness. Perfectionists are locked inside a world of "shoulds," expectations, and obligations fanning the flames and drive toward the next achievement. The only reward is a brief sense of accomplishment before they burst into goal-oriented activity again.

Perfectionism is mainly driven by fear – the fear of failure. Even partial failure means complete and total failure to the perfectionist. To the outside world, perfectionists may appear to be successful, accomplished, and have it all together. They may be well-respected by their peers and in the community, but underneath that polished and put-together veneer is insecurity, and the fear of rejection and abandonment. Perfectionism is the ultimate defense mechanism for emotionally abandoned children.

There are three types of perfectionists:

1. *Inward focused* – have high expectations of themselves for achieving, doing better, and being the best.

2. *Outward focused* – have high expectations of others and are hard on them when they fail to meet these expectations.

57

3. *Expectations perceived to come from others* – social standards drive the need for perfection. Social media is a big influence on the need to appear perfect.

Rates of perfectionism and the need to be perfect have soared with young people over the last 30 years. Studies show perfectionism in youth is connected to higher rates of depression, anxiety, eating disorders, and suicidal ideation. Social media most likely plays a big part in pressuring teens to look perfect for selfies and posts to their social pages. Appearing to be perfect provides a feeling of safety, and the connection socially gives them the validation of their worthiness.

Are You a Perfectionist?

Answer yes or no to the following questions to determine the level of perfectionist qualities you have:

1. I am completely aware of and critical of mistakes – mine or others.

2. I try to be the best in everything I do, even if it's something I'm not really interested in.

3. My ideals and beliefs tend to be rigid, black and white with no grey area.

4. I tend to be my worst critic.

5. I spend a great deal of time perfecting things, at the expense of my health and leisure time.

6. I have an all-or-nothing way of doing things.

7. I focus on the outcome and don't really pay attention to or enjoy the journey.

8. I tend to dwell on results or mistakes if things didn't turn out the way I wanted.

9. I get defensive when receiving criticism from others and fear failure.

10. I procrastinate or avoid situations that could tip people off that I'm not perfect.

11. I don't trust other people to do things the "right way."

12. I have high expectations of myself.

13. I have high expectations of others.

14. I have difficulty finishing projects because it seems there are always more ways to improve them.

15. "Should" is a frequent word in my vocabulary.

16. I feel good about myself when I accomplish something and receive validation from others.

17. I tend to fixate on what I can do better.

18. I won't even try something if I think I'm not good at it.

19. I do things out of expectation or a sense of obligation.

20. I tend to think and act in extremes.

OK, so how did it go? There's no right or wrong answer – this was just a tool for you to become aware of whether you have perfectionist tendencies. Some perfectionism is actually quite healthy. It gives you the drive to achieve a goal or do something well. Taking on a challenge and succeeding is rewarding and feels great. We don't always want to play it safe and stay on the sidelines, so some perfectionism is helpful in getting out of your comfort zone and achieving something important to you. Too much perfectionism, however, leads to fear of failure and avoidance behaviors such as procrastination, and that definitely does not feel great.

What is the cost of perfectionism?

1. *Procrastination* – putting off getting things done due to fear of failure.

2. *Less productive and put in more work* – spending more time on projects to make them perfect, and that time could be spent on getting other important things done.

3. ***Constant stress*** – feeling under the pressure to constantly perform perfectly takes a toll on the mind, body, emotions, and spirit.

4. ***Never-ending dissatisfaction and unhappiness*** – perfection is never attainable since things are never good enough or perfect enough.

Perfectionism is an impossible paradox. First, because perfection can never be achieved, and second, because everything is already perfect just the way it is right now. The only way to win at the game of perfection, to achieve perfection, is to let go of the fear that drives it. Let go of the fear of rejection, abandonment, and unworthiness and see the beauty and perfection in everything in this moment. The present moment is perfect, it can't be changed or improved on because it already is. Perfectionists like to think in terms of future scenarios because that's where the hope for love and acceptance lives. By bringing attention and awareness into the present moment, it's easier to recognize that reality is perfectly imperfect.

So, how do you beat perfectionism and get to the present moment?

1. ***Challenge the inner critic*** – Just like with toxic shame, begin challenging the negative thoughts and words you think and say about yourself. You can say or think something like, "Thanks, but I don't believe that about myself anymore," "I did my best

61

and I'm satisfied with my work," or "I don't need to do or be anything in order to be worthy of love."

2. *Accept reality the way it is* – This one is difficult for perfectionists because of the desire to perpetually change how things are. Expecting reality to be different than it is leads to struggle and suffering. Acceptance is the absence of judgment and comparison. It may feel radical at first, but accepting things the way they are ends suffering and leads to peace. The mindfulness activities in section two provide guidance on getting to acceptance.

3. *Identify emotional triggers* – When the urge for perfection arises, ask yourself what you really need. Perfectionism is a childhood response to trauma and distracts from feeling painful emotions. When you can identify the emotions, be like a scientist and observe them without attachment, such as, "Hmm, interesting, I'm feeling anxious and worried about trying this new thing and I don't want to fail at it." Once you observe what's happening, remind yourself that you're safe and all is well. Emotions can feel like life or death, but they're just emotions; in the past, you avoided feeling them through doing and achieving. Acknowledge and accept the feeling and let it go. Once you have worked

through the emotional triggers, the need for perfectionism no longer exists. The feel and heal activities in section two provide guidance for processing emotions.

4. ***Move into self-compassion*** – This is the final step in managing perfectionism. Self-compassion allows you to see yourself as a human being, who by their very nature are perfectly imperfect. It gives you permission to try new things, make mistakes, and learn and grow from them. Incorporating compassion for yourself provides the perfect balance of allowing yourself some grace while you go through life, but not making excuses and letting yourself off the hook all the time. Moving Into the Heart in section two provides exercises to incorporate self-compassion into your life.

Chapter 6

Addictions and Trauma

"Turn your face to the sun and the shadows fall

behind you." – Charlotte Whitton

My brother and I went to visit our grandparents in North Carolina every summer for two weeks. We typically spent one of those weeks traveling to various locations in the South, like Washington DC or Myrtle Beach. It was 1980 and my brother and I were riding in the back of the Cadillac. I was nine years old and had a little notebook with me where I wrote down some goals I had for the trip. It went something like this: "Lose 10 pounds by eating only Grapenuts, see the Smithsonian, say hi to the president." I was normally ecstatic when we got to visit my grandparents because they always stocked the pantry with our favorite sugar cereals, cookies, and snacks that we never got to have at home. I would stuff myself with Fruity Pebbles, Cocoa Puffs, and Chocolate Chip Archway Cookies, and I was in total heaven.

That year was different though. My parents had been fighting nonstop (which wasn't that unusual), they split up, and my dad had moved out. I guess maybe I thought if I ate healthy that I could fix things. Despite my determination and vow to make things right, as soon as we stopped at a rest area, I gobbled down a homemade lunch of egg salad and Nacho Cheese Doritos. That wasn't enough for me though because I went to the restroom and washed out my Styrofoam cup so I could put Doritos in it and eat them in the car. My grandmother was onto me though and had me put the cup in the trunk for later. That was the beginning of my 30 year-long battle with restricting my food and then later bingeing to soothe my nerves.

I was a stress eater. I used food to numb the emotional pain or to soothe my anxiety, and then exercised so I wouldn't gain weight. I tried dieting and restricting my food, but that only worked in times of extreme shame or self-loathing, and even then, I usually went shopping to fill the void where the food had been. I didn't understand that my sympathetic nervous system was on overdrive, and that the only way I could stop soothing myself with food was to address the underlying trauma issues. Once I understood that, I then had to learn how to stop using food to deal with the painful trauma memories I was working through. It was a long, difficult, and exhausting journey, but eventually I made it to a place of self-acceptance and peace around food and my body. I learned how to handle difficult situations and emotions without numbing or soothing, and I was able to stay present while holding a loving space for my body to take the time it needed to heal.

It is generally accepted now that addiction is often a result of unresolved trauma. Children of an alcoholic parent, particularly women, are 70 percent more likely to develop an addiction to sugar resulting in an eating disorder, than children of non-alcoholics. Studies have shown that a child who experiences four or more adverse childhood experiences (ACEs) is five times more likely to become an alcoholic, 60 percent more likely to become obese, and an astounding forty-six times more likely to become addicted to injection drugs, than the general population. The Veterans Administration estimates that between 35 percent to 75 percent of veterans with PTSD abuse drugs and alcohol. Early trauma can impact a person's ability to deal with stress. High levels of stress as a child prevented the brain from developing properly, and this creates a vulnerability to substance abuse later in life. When the stress becomes too overwhelming, it usually leads to addiction in some form or another.

As mentioned earlier, the consequences of unresolved trauma can result in serious long-term problems. PTSD can have a devastating impact on relationships, careers, emotions, physical and mental health, families, and behaviors. Symptoms of PTSD include flashbacks, nightmares, sleep issues, anxiety and depression, dissociation and a disconnect from reality, excessive fears, impulsiveness, and a predisposition to addiction. Oftentimes, individuals will self-medicate in an attempt to manage their PTSD symptoms. Substance abuse often leads to risky behaviors, which put the individual in re-traumatizing situations, creating the need to self-medicate even more. The daily struggle to keep trauma memories away is exhausting, and results in feelings of isolation, vulnerability, and aloneness.

Once a person gets clean and sober, if they've been using substances to numb the memories of trauma and those memories are still repressed and unresolved, they often end up trading one addiction for another. For example, a recovering alcoholic may substitute nicotine, caffeine, or sugar as a replacement for alcohol. It's not possible to address trauma while still in active addiction, and the harmful effects of chronic exposure to experiences of abuse and neglect can run deep, so it's a delicate balance between staying sober while healing the trauma so that sobriety can be maintained.

First and foremost, a feeling of safety and stability must be achieved. Things might feel worse at first before they start getting better. Because trauma and addiction often create feelings of isolation, recovery needs to include healthy connections, forgiveness of self and others, acceptance, and establishing trust and safety in relationships.

Most addiction treatment centers recognize the need for integrated treatment for both addiction and trauma since over two-thirds of people with addictions have also experienced trauma.

I wanted to include a chapter on addiction because of the correlation between addiction and trauma, but I'm not going to go into detail about treatment for addiction since hundreds of books are written on this topic. There are also tons of modalities available for addressing addictions. The ones that I've found to be particularly helpful when addressing both trauma and addiction are mindfulness-based practices such as meditation and yoga, dialectic behavioral therapy (DBT), eye movement desensitization and reprocessing (EMDR), emotional freedom technique (EFT), hypnosis, neurofeedback, and somatic experiencing (SE). I've included some helpful links in the resources section for additional information on these modalities. Some of the exercises in section two of this book can also help with addictions.

Section II:

Overcoming Trauma

Chapter 7

The 8 Steps

"It is by going down into the abyss that we recover the treasures of life. Where you stumble, there lies your treasure." – Joseph Campbell

I wanted to be a shaman. When I started on my spiritual journey, I attended workshops, retreats, and classes on healing, psychic development, crystals, flower essences, law of attraction, angels, the energy field, and past life regression. I was hungry for information and signed up for everything that was of interest to me. It seemed that as soon as I wanted to learn something, the class or teacher appeared for me. It was an intense but very enjoyable time. I connected with like-minded people and felt like I was part of a community – something that I hadn't felt in a very long time. It was a deeply healing and transformational process. Like many people, once I started feeling better, I wanted to help others heal, so I became certified in over twenty different healing modalities and opened a private practice. I became a Reiki master, clinical hypnotherapist, spiritual counselor, and angel intuitive (a certification program by Doreen Virtue that no longer exists).

During that period of accelerated spiritual learning, I went to see a woman who did readings by channeling one of her guides. At the time, I was studying with a shaman and really admired how powerful, intuitive, and connected to the earth she was. I decided that I wanted to be a shaman too, which required a big investment of time and money, so I wanted to receive guidance on this decision. Three things came out of that reading. First, I could go the shaman route although it didn't particularly line up with my energy; it wasn't a bad thing and there's free will and all, so it was up to me. Second, I traveled with a fleet of angels. When I asked her more about that she said, "You're special." Not in the magical way of being special though, like I wanted that to mean, but the kind of special that needs extra help through dark times. I replied, "Yeah, I had a tough go a while back with some suicide attempts and depression, but everyone goes through the dark night of the soul and things are good now." The third takeaway from that meeting was that I hadn't seen the last of those dark times, and that it was part of my calling to help others.

I set that information aside for several years and threw myself into working with clients and teaching Reiki and meditation at the local college. I created a holistic practitioner certification program and trained and certified healing practitioners. I loved what I was doing and continued taking more classes to expand my healing work. I studied medical intuition because I noticed when I did energy work on people, I began picking up on health issues in their bodies, so I wanted to understand that better. I studied mediumship because people would bring spirit attachments into sessions, and I needed to learn how to release them and cross them over. Clients' deceased loved ones also showed up in sessions and I began communicating those messages to them. I was also getting requests for space clearings of homes and businesses, so I learned to work with the energies of land and homes.

As I continued to deepen my knowledge and healing capabilities, I noticed that the clients I was working with had heavy trauma issues like sexual abuse, assaults, or domestic violence. About a year into working with these clients' trauma issues, I became extremely fatigued, burned out, and depressed. I tried to push my way through because I was on a mission to save the world, but I could barely function and was diagnosed with fibromyalgia and chronic fatigue. I closed my practice and began to focus once more on healing myself. I later learned that what I had experienced was vicarious trauma – I was taking on their traumas and processing them through my own body like they were my own.

Apparently, my spirit likes to take deep dives into the dark to learn. Working with trauma clients had triggered my own buried trauma and it took a toll on my body, mind, spirit, and emotions. I began having flashbacks, nightmares, and chronic, unexplained pain in my body. I didn't sleep well, and had constant panic attacks, sometimes more than once a day. I spent time huddled in my closet, because that felt like the only safe place for me. I vacillated between rage and despair and contemplated suicide daily. I felt misunderstood, hopeless, lost, and didn't have the resources I needed to deal with my symptoms. It was a dark and lonely period in my life, and I honestly didn't think I would come back from it this time.

Somehow though, I kept going. My angels must have stayed by my side, nudging me and guiding me as I stumbled around in the dark looking for answers. Over the next five years, I threw myself into my own healing and studied everything I could about trauma. I earned my master's degree in psychology with a specialization in trauma and crisis response. I went to specialists who helped me release the trauma from my body. I learned dialectal behavior therapy (DBT), which helped me regulate my emotions, manage my response to discomfort, and relate with people better on an interpersonal level. I began incorporating mindfulness practices to soothe my sympathetic nervous system and ground myself when I dissociated. It wasn't an easy process and I got stuck for weeks or months at a time. Trauma healing can feel like two steps forward and then ten steps backward sometimes. I cried, I cursed the heavens, and I railed against the injustice of these difficult lessons. Why couldn't I have had a nice, simple, and peaceful life in Greece?

But I kept moving forward and eventually, I found that certain triggers no longer bothered me. My heart rate began to slow down, and the unexplained pain left my body. I felt like I was through the worst of it. Then out of the blue, my left knee began blowing up almost weekly with inflammation and fluid, and I knew I had more work to do. I dove into forgiveness practices, especially those of self-forgiveness. I had done forgiveness work years before and thought I was done with it. I forgave people easily, but what I was holding on to was the hurt and feelings of betrayal. I thought I needed those to justify my pain and what had been done to me, and if I didn't have them, what did I have left? Maybe I was still holding out for an apology or acknowledgment of what happened. I was only hurting myself by hanging on, so it was finally time to let them go, and I practiced forgiveness like my life depended on it.

I began incorporating self-love into my daily routine, which included self-compassion and self-care. At first, I had no idea what those even meant. I heard people talk about them and I even prescribed them to my clients, but I didn't know what it *really* meant for me. I could do them for a while, but when I was triggered, I couldn't stick to it. Everything went out the window and I went back to my old coping mechanisms, like emotional eating or busyness. I realized that it was during those times that I needed self-love the most! As soon as I made the commitment to myself to practice self-love, *especially when I was triggered*, things really started falling into place like the missing pieces of a puzzle. I started waking up each day excited to begin my morning practices, filled with gratitude and an abundance of energy for the new day. It had been years since I felt anything remotely close to this and back then it was usually fueled by caffeine or Adderall. This feeling was natural and on an entirely new level. I started receiving guidance on the next steps of my journey, and I began putting together a trauma healing program based on practices and tools that worked for me. That is how the 8 Steps to Overcoming Trauma were created.

I never imagined I would be teaching and writing about trauma. I always envisioned my first book to be about angels or energy healing, something light and easy that would make people feel warm and fuzzy inside after reading. I mean I certainly didn't think I'd be the one taking a deep dive into the bowels of hell, walking through the fire of trauma, and emerging from the journey wiping the soot of darkness out of my eyes while hollering, "Hey, I've got something cool to share with you!" I really thought about sidestepping the topic and addressing it in a covert way that had a spiritual title but was really about trauma, but that isn't really my style. No, my gifts are being able to understand something deeply and intricately (often via trial by fire), gathering the information and tools needed, and then organizing and presenting it in a way that's easy to use and understand. The 8 steps that I found to be the most helpful for healing trauma and giving you back your life so you can find happiness and peace within are:

Step 1: Building Resilience

Step 2: Raising Your Vibration

Step 3: Managing Your Thoughts

Step 4: Feeling Leads to Healing

Step 5: Moving Into the Heart

Step 6: Forgiveness and Letting Go

Step 7: Self-Love and Self-Care

Step 8: Keep Moving Forward

I have intentionally arranged the 8 steps in an order where each step builds on one another, and as you strengthen the skills in one area, you move on to the next. There is no right or wrong way to follow the steps, and you can jump around these chapters if you wish. Keep in mind that it might be difficult to leap straight into forgiveness, if you are still working through trauma symptoms or if you haven't processed difficult emotions. Take your time with each step and work at a pace that's comfortable for you. Some people go back through the steps over and over to reinforce the skills and stay consistent with their daily practices. I definitely recommend creating a strong, consistent daily practice. It doesn't have to be perfect, of course, but consistency is crucial. That's how you will build resilience and manage day-to-day stress or triggers without feeling overwhelmed or sucked under by heavy emotions. I've included examples of daily routines in the chapter on continuing to move forward in the healing process. If you are working through the steps on your own and find that you are getting triggered during this process, you may need the support of a therapist or trauma professional. I have included some links in the additional resources section to help you find assistance, if needed.

You are probably more than ready to get started, so let's do this.

Chapter 8

Step 1 – Building Resilience

"Man never made any material as resilient as the

human spirit." – Bernard Williams

People often said to me, "You're so strong" or "I could never have made it through that." The truth is that I didn't feel strong. Not. At. All. I feel that you should get rewarded for just surviving trauma. Like a get-out-of-jail-free card where you get to bypass all the crappy stuff and live a great life from that point on. But then again, I also feel like you should get to lose weight when you pass up on eating something delicious and you shouldn't have to get your period every month if you're not having sex. Those are just some of the rules of the universe I would have included had I been around and consulted when things were being created. Obviously, there's a reason I'm not in charge of the big stuff.

Dealing with the after-effects of unresolved trauma years or decades later, and often after being retraumatized multiple times over, is not for the faint of heart, and in my opinion, deserves the grand prize of all prizes. However, since this is the school of life and not a game show, and we came here to learn and evolve, the consolation prize that we get for participating in it is resilience. Human beings are unbelievably resilient and are wired for survival. But I always wondered why is it that some people bounce back from trauma easily while others are absolutely devastated by it?

Resilience is how well we adapt when we are faced with difficulties such as trauma, loss, or other extremely stressful experiences. It's how we are able to bounce back from adversity. Studies show that resilience is an inherent trait in everyone, and that people demonstrate resilience all the time. Stress and difficulties are often an unavoidable part of life. How we handle those experiences reflects our level of resilience. We learn resilience from our primary caregivers, by watching how they handle stressful situations and how they overcome difficulties through their behaviors and actions.

People who handle difficulties well have several factors in common. The main factor is the presence of caring and supportive relationships. Relationships that foster love and trust, offer role models, and provide encouragement and reassurance, which increase resilience.

Other factors for resilience are managing strong feelings and impulses, confidence in one's abilities and strengths, good communication and problem-solving skills, and making realistic plans and carrying them out. Unfortunately, people who have experienced trauma, especially prolonged exposure to trauma in childhood, most likely didn't have the best role models or loving relationships, and their under-developed brains put them at a disadvantage for developing these skills. The great news is that we can develop these skills within ourselves at any time.

Ten ways we can build resilience:

1. **Connect with others** – Isolation is common when struggling with symptoms of trauma. By connecting with others, we're able to create supportive and loving relationships that strengthen our resilience and get us through tough times.

2. **Believe that you can overcome it** – When we're in the thick of things, it's hard to see a way out. Knowing that you have successfully dealt with challenges in the past will help bolster your confidence in overcoming this situation too.

3. **Acceptance** – We know that things are easier to deal with when we accept them. Denying the problem or wishing it wasn't there won't get you any closer to resolving it. Accepting something for what it is can be a powerful step toward overcoming it.

4. **Increase self-awareness** – Knowing your triggers and potential trip ups is useful when dealing with times of high stress or difficulties. You can create a backup plan or call in support when needed.

5. **Stay hopeful** – There is always a way out or through. Trust in yourself and your abilities to handle anything that comes your way.

6. **Self-care** – When you take care of yourself, you're better able to manage stressful situations. This involves getting enough sleep, feeding yourself right, and taking time to rest.

7. **Develop confidence in yourself** – When you trust yourself and believe in your abilities, you know you can handle whatever curveball life throws at you.

8. **See things from a different perspective** – This one is tricky sometimes when you're in the middle of it. But if you can step out of your situation and view it as an observer, not a participant, you can gain a new perspective, and often the situation doesn't seem so bad.

9. **Take inspired action** – When you take action, it gives your brain something to focus on rather than dwelling on the problem. Inspired action is intentional and purposeful.

10. **Keep moving forward** – Making forward progress is an
    absolute game-changer for building resilience. As you get some
    wins under your belt and you've successfully handled a few
    challenges, your confidence builds, and the momentum carries
    you forward into a world of new possibilities.

Exercises for Building Resilience

Breathwork

This is going to be an important exercise as you begin to build
your resilience. People who have experienced trauma or are under
chronic, high levels of stress tend to have very short, shallow breathing.
I don't know why it's called breath*work* because it is one of the quickest
and easiest ways to calm your nerves, energize, and center yourself.
Pranayama is a yogic term for control over the energy in the breath.
It provides quick and efficient ways to tap into the nervous system.
Research has shown how breathwork relieves stress and anxiety and
helps with trauma recovery.

Calming Breath: Use this before bed, at work, or anytime you need
to calm your nervous system. How to do it: Place one hand on your
heart and one hand on your belly. Inhale through the nose counting
to five, then exhale through the nose counting to five. Make sure that
the breath is going through the diaphragm into the belly, and not the

chest. You'll feel the rise and fall of your belly as you breathe in and out. Repeat for a minimum of 3 minutes.

Alternate Nostril Breathing: This type of breathing calms, balances, and unites the right and left sides of the brain. It's great for releasing fatigue and tension. <u>How to do it:</u> Start in a comfortable meditative pose, hold the right thumb over the right nostril and inhale deeply through the left nostril. At the peak of inhalation, close off the left nostril with the ring finger, then exhale through the right nostril. Continue the pattern, inhaling through the right nostril, closing it off with the right thumb, and exhaling through the left nostril.

15-Second Breath: This breathing exercise soothes fear and helps with cognition. <u>How to do it:</u> Begin by inhaling slowly for 5 seconds, filling the lower abdomen, stomach area, lungs, and then finally, the chest. Hold the breath in for 5 seconds and then slowly exhale for 5 seconds. Increase the number of seconds counting 10-10-10 when you feel comfortable. Do for a minimum of 3 minutes.

Dragon Breath: This is an energizing breathing technique and great when you wake up in the morning. <u>How to do it:</u> Begin in a comfortable seat and sit up tall. Breathe through your nose during this breathing exercise. Relax the muscles of the stomach. Take a deep inhalation through the nose and then exhale through the nose. Begin to breathe rapidly in and out through the nose and pump the navel point in and out with each breath. Maintain an equal emphasis on the exhalation and inhalation. The breath should be shallow, so it can be quick. Caution: this is an energizing exercise – if you are already experiencing high stress, rapid heart rate, or anxiety, choose one of the calming breathing techniques above.

Mindfulness Exercises

In 1979, Jon Kabat-Zinn began studying the effectiveness of mindfulness for stress relief. He recruited individuals who had chronic pain and were not responding to other forms of treatment. It was an eight week program for stress reduction, which was later called mindfulness-based stress reduction (MBSR). Since that time, a mountain of data has shown that MBSR has a positive and lasting effect on improving mental and physical health. Incorporating mindfulness-based practices for individuals with trauma and high-stress experiences has been shown to strengthen emotion regulation, create more awareness of the physical body, and reduce the occurrence of dissociation, a protective mechanism as a way of "detaching," in times of high stress or when triggered emotionally. In addition to helping with managing stress associated with chronic pain, MBSR has been helpful for anxiety disorders and depression, often associated with PTSD. Mindfulness builds more connections in the brain that slow down the reactiveness of the sympathetic nervous system. Paying attention in the present moment changes the structure and rewires functions in the brain.

Using mindfulness is a way to bring your awareness into the present moment, and to intentionally pay attention through nonjudgment to what is going on inside and around you. When just starting out with mindfulness practices, it is best to begin slowly. Some people are OK with sitting quietly for long periods of time, while others are not. The great thing about these exercises is that they are very short and easy to do. However, they are also very effective! You only need 5 to 10 minutes a day for you to notice a difference in how you feel, and I often do these while I'm out and about if I need to. You can use these practices whenever and wherever works for you.

Orienting: This is very helpful when you are feeling triggered and if you dissociate when triggered. Orienting is used in somatic experiencing, a trauma healing process developed by Peter Levine. It's based on the idea that when an animal is in its environment and senses a threat, it determines whether the threat is real or not by looking around and scanning the area. People with trauma are typically on constant high alert and everything can feel threatening. The process of moving the head and the neck to scan around you, allows the limbic brain and nerves on the back of the neck to realize that all is well and it's OK to relax. How to do it: Sit comfortably in a chair and with your eyes open, slowly turn your head all the way to the left and notice what's there. Then slowly move your head all the way to the right and notice what's in that direction. Slowly, look up and then down, paying attention to what you see. Finally, slowly turn your head to see what's behind you. Do everything intentionally, slowly, and don't push past any tension or pain. Be an observer of what you notice, "Hmm, interesting ... there's a lamp." Do this for a few minutes each day.

Orienting with Senses: This mindfulness exercise allows you to bring your awareness to your body and the present moment through the senses. It is a great one to use when you're feeling triggered or if you frequently dissociate. <u>How to do it:</u> You can do this exercise pretty much anywhere – while sitting in a chair, driving, shopping, at work. Slowly bring your awareness to your body. Notice what you are seeing in that moment, "I see that tree." Then notice what you hear, "I hear music playing." Then notice what you feel (sensorily, not emotionally), "I feel my keys in my hand" or "I feel my feet in my shoes." Do this with the other senses: taste and smell. You may have to repeat the process once or twice to stay present and focused in the moment. Practice this exercise daily.

Mindful or Meditative Yoga

There has been increasing awareness regarding how yoga can aid in healing trauma. Bessel Van der Kolk, a leading trauma researcher, recommends incorporating mindful or meditative yoga into trauma treatment. There are several reasons for this. First, traumatized people often get stuck in powerlessness because they were unable to or were prevented from taking action at the time of the trauma, such as fighting or fleeing, and their body needs to complete the action. Second, dissociation is a common symptom of trauma and creates a disconnect from the body. People with trauma need to reconnect with the sensations in the body and release trapped energies and emotions connected to the trauma. Finally, trauma survivors' bodies get taken over when triggered by loud sounds, criticism, or hurtful things, and they need to engage the body in a mindful way in order to release stress hormones and reset the critical areas of the brain. Mindful or meditative yoga is a way to calm the mind and feel safe and present in the body.

The main goal of this type of yoga is that it engages the body in a mindful way. Trauma-sensitive yoga, mindful yoga therapy, qigong, and meditative flow are some types of movement that can provide trauma healing through mindful movement. I've included some links in the resources section for information. Also, there is a link to a 7-minute meditative flow yoga video you can follow to give this type of yoga a try. This was perfect for me in the beginning because I was totally resistant to yoga in the first place, and my excuse was always that I didn't have enough time. Well, 7 minutes is easy to make time for, and I loved how I felt afterward, especially in such a short amount of time!

Meditation

Similar to the studies on mindfulness, there has been a lot of research on the effects of meditation on healing trauma. An increasing amount of data shows the positive outcome of meditation on the brain. Brain scans show that meditation helps slow down and reduce grey matter in the overactive amygdala, and strengthens the prefrontal cortex and hippocampus, actually increasing grey matter in these underdeveloped areas of the brain. So, in other words, meditation reverses the effects that trauma had on the brain.

Some meditations are more beneficial than others in trauma healing. Some people may feel triggered in quiet meditation that lasts for longer periods of time. It's best to start slow and with mindfulness meditations such as counting breaths, or progressive relaxation that focuses on relaxing different parts of the body one at a time. Guided meditations are helpful as well, especially if you are new to meditation and don't know where to start. There's no right or wrong way to meditate, the point is to just try to work in some time for mindfulness.

Some of the most common features in mindfulness meditation include:

• **Focusing your attention**. Focusing your attention is generally one of the most important elements of meditation. Focusing your attention is what helps free your mind from the many distractions that cause stress and worry. You can focus your attention on such things as a specific object, an image, a mantra, or even your breathing. There's no need to worry when your mind wanders. Just return to your focus of attention.

• **Relaxed breathing**. Most people with high stress levels take short, shallow breaths. Relaxed breathing involves deep, even-paced breathing using the diaphragm muscle to expand your lungs. The purpose is to slow your breathing, take in more oxygen, and reduce the use of shoulder, neck, and upper chest muscles while breathing so that you breathe more efficiently. Belly breaths are another way to practice relaxed breathing. Instead of taking air into the chest, you take it into your belly and allow it to rise and fall naturally.

• **A quiet location**. If you're a beginner, practicing meditation may be easier if you're in a quiet spot with few distractions – no television, radios, or cell phones. As you get more skilled at meditation, you may be able to do it anywhere, especially in high-stress situations where you benefit the most from meditation, such as a traffic jam, a stressful work meeting, or a long line at the grocery store.

• **A comfortable position**. You can practice meditation whether you're sitting, lying down, walking, or in other positions, or during certain activities. Many people prefer sitting to lying down because they tend to fall asleep lying down. Whatever you choose, the main goal is to be comfortable so that you can get the most out of your meditation.

Here are some simple mindfulness meditations to start with:

Count Your Breaths: The breath is the focus of this meditation. Try to focus on the rhythm of your breathing. To make your focus easier, you'll count every breath in and every breath out. Every time your mind wanders, simply return your focus to your breathing and begin counting again. <u>How to do it:</u> In a relaxed seated position, begin to focus on your breaths, breathing in and out naturally. Notice the sensations of your breath as you inhale and exhale. You can breathe in and out through your nose or in through your nose and out through your mouth, whatever is more comfortable for you. Begin to count your breaths ... inhale 1 ... exhale 2 ... inhale 3 ... exhale 4 ... If your mind wanders, just bring your counting back to 1 and begin again. Do this for 5 to 10 minutes daily and increase the time at whatever pace feels comfortable to you.

Mantra Meditation: With this meditation, a sound, a word, a sentence, or an affirmation is the focus of your meditation. Similar to counting breaths, you'll focus your attention on the word or words of your mantra. <u>How to do it:</u> Choose a mantra that has meaning for you. In a relaxed seated position, begin to focus on your mantra. You can repeat the words quietly in your mind or out loud, whichever you prefer. You can sync the words to your breaths if you wish. For example, if your mantra is "letting go" you can breathe in to "letting" and breathe out "go." Do this for 5 to 10 minutes daily and increase the time at whatever pace feels comfortable to you.

Guided Meditations: These are great to begin with because you can just sit or lay down while listening to someone else guiding you through the meditation. Guided meditations can come in many different formats and cover a variety of topics from relaxation to healing to spiritual journeys. You may find as you try out different guided meditations, that you like some people's voices, or music, or style better than others. I have a couple of dozen of my favorites and rotate what I listen to depending on my mood or needs at the time.

Chapter 9

Step 2 – Raising Your Vibration

"It is not easy to find happiness in ourselves, and it is not possible to find it elsewhere." – Agnes Repplier

I
t took years for me to learn how to pull myself out of depression, fear, lethargy, or anxiety for any sustained period of time. I would often stay in those states for days, weeks, or even months sometimes, unable to even get to a place of neutrality or catch a glimpse of easier times ahead. Feeling peace, joy, or happiness wasn't on my radar at all back then. I frequently woke up triggered and full of self-loathing and felt alone, hopeless, and wanting to die. I never understood how closely related shame and self-loathing are to despair and death, until I read *Power vs Force* by David Hawkins. Hawkins used muscle testing, a form of kinesiology, to determine levels of consciousness and rated them on a scale of 0 to 1,000, with 17 different levels of consciousness on the scale. As individuals move up the scale, their life view begins to shift from one that is fear-based

to that of love. Hawkins's "Map of Consciousness" provides scientific documentation and a new level of understanding of the mystical and spiritual journey of human evolution. The scale indicates the vibrational frequency of things, and Hawkins tested the calibration of thousands of items – emotions and attitudes, worldviews, politics, religions, rituals such as lighting incense or saying a prayer, and gatherings of people in worship, prayer, and AA meetings.

The scale of consciousness rates different levels of awareness, the emotions, and the life view associated with them. There is a critical point on the scale at the 200 mark, which is the level of *courage*, that balances between higher/lower consciousness, strength/weakness, and power/force. Attitudes, thoughts, and feelings that calibrate over 200, help an individual move up the scale, while those that calibrate below 200, keep an individual stuck in negativity and lower consciousness. At the time he did the testing, Hawkins determined that humanity on average calibrated at just over 200 at 204. Of course, some people have a vibrational frequency much higher than this, and many people much lower. What I found really interesting in Hawkins's work is that one person who vibrates at 350 can counteract 200,000 people calibrating below 200, and a person who calibrates at the 500 level counteracts over 750,000 vibrating under 200. Here's the Map of Consciousness that Hawkins created:

Levels of Consciousness:

God-View	Life-View	Level	Log	Emotion	Process	
Self	Is	ENLIGHTENMENT	700-1000	Ineffable	Pure Consciousness	
All-Being	Perfect	PEACE	600	Bliss	Illumination	
One	Complete	JOY	540	Serenity	Transfiguration	
Loving	Benign	LOVE	500	Reverence	Revelation	POWER
Wise	Meaningful	REASON	400	Understanding	Abstraction	
Merciful	Harmonious	ACCEPTANCE	350	Forgiveness	Transcendence	
Inspiring	Hopeful	WILLINGNESS	310	Optimism	Intention	
Enabling	Satisfactory	NEUTRALITY	250	Trust	Release	
Permitting	Feasible	COURAGE	200	Affirmation	Empowerment	
Indifferent	Demanding	PRIDE	175	Scorn	Inflation	
Vengeful	Antagonistic	ANGER	150	Hate	Aggression	
Denying	Disappointing	DESIRE	125	Craving	Enslavement	FORCE
Punitive	Frightening	FEAR	75	Anxiety	Withdrawal	
Disdainful	Tragic	GRIEF	75	Regret	Despondency	
Condemning	Hopeless	APATHY	50	Despair	Abdication	
Vindictive	Evil	GUILT	30	Blame	Destruction	
Despise	Miserable	SHAME	20	Humiliation	Elimination	

People who are struggling with the devastating effects and symptoms of trauma tend to get stuck in these lower levels, and have a difficult time finding their way out of them. I unconsciously worked my way up and down the lower levels by default with knee-jerk reactions to triggers, impulsiveness, intolerance to discomfort, feeling like a victim and blaming others, or numbing the emotional and physical pain with food. Living for years with toxic shame and waking up in self-loathing kept me vibrating at the very lowest level, and it's not a surprise that I was miserable and wanting to die.

Trauma affects the mind, body, spirit, and emotions, disrupting the natural processes of the brain and body, creating negative thoughts, patterns, habits, and beliefs. This perpetuates the cycle of people remaining stuck in these lower vibrations. When I started using the steps that I've outlined in this book, I began to *consciously* work my way up the scale and increase my level of consciousness. I was also able to maintain these higher levels for longer periods of time, whereas before I could only get a brief glimpse of a better feeling, and then I'd end up right back down in a lower consciousness again. As my skills developed, if my vibration dropped in response to the actions of other people or outside events, I could quickly bring myself back to center using these tools, raising my vibration to a higher level of consciousness.

It is empowering to learn that you have control over your responses to other people's words and actions, as well as to challenging events and situations. Trauma survivors often feel like victims, that life happens to them, and powerless to the world around them. Although it does take practice, discipline, and consistency to master the skills needed in order to calibrate over 200 for extended periods of time, even just the slightest shift up the scale can make a profound difference. For example, if you've been stuck in depression, or the freeze trauma response, and have had a difficult time getting even the most basic tasks done each day, getting angry about something would be beneficial to you. Even though anger is a lower level consciousness, it calibrates three times higher on the scale than apathy. Getting angry would raise your vibration and help you with the energy necessary to take action. Anger provides the much-needed fuel for the fire for the motivation and drive to reach goals or achieve desires. However, it's important not to stay in anger too long or it can lead to resentment, judgment, or turn inward leading back down the scale to guilt and shame. There are more positive ways to ignite your fire and raise your vibration, and I've included those exercises at the end of this chapter.

The Map of Consciousness provides a great tool for awareness and a guide to understanding the level you're at now and where you'd like to be in the future, and places the power in your hands, knowing that you have control over where you calibrate on the scale. Occasionally, I'll get angry or upset about something, and I have all the tools I need to shift out of it and quickly raise my vibration, but I'll choose to sit in that anger for a day or two, feeling justified or just wanting to stew for a bit. After a while, I realize I don't want to be in that lower vibration anymore, and I use the steps to raise myself out of it. The difference between my old knee-jerk reactions to triggers and now, is that I felt like I couldn't control my responses before. Now I'm consciously aware of where I'm at, and it's my choice to sit in a lower vibration for a while.

Once you've been hanging out in the higher vibrational frequencies for a while, it doesn't feel very good to spend much time in the lower vibrations, so you might find that you move out of it much more quickly than you used to! As you raise your vibration, you may discover that your preferences for things may change, or that you can't tolerate certain things anymore. A few years ago, I bought tickets to one of my favorite bands from the 1990s and I ended up leaving the concert because it didn't resonate with my energy anymore. The music made me edgy and irritable. There are also certain foods such as flour, sugar, wheat, and other processed foods that my body can't tolerate anymore, and I avoid mood-altering substances like alcohol, caffeine, and stimulants. Occasionally I'll eat or drink something that I used to love and have all the time, and it doesn't feel good at all, and it really bums me out, but it's just not worth the discomfort to ingest those lower vibrating things anymore. I'm also much more clear-headed and in tune with everything when I refrain from indulging in those items!

Another valuable tool for elevating your vibration is the law of attraction. When people hear about the law of attraction, they tend to think of manifesting material things, like a new car or money. However, the law of attraction can be used for healing and to work your way up the levels of consciousness. Skeptics may think of the law of attraction as some absurd, new age impossible woo-woo magic. I love that the

100

movie *The Secret* brought awareness of the law of attraction to the general population and provided people with an understanding of how it works. I felt it was a little too focused on manifesting wealth or material items, and it left out what a huge impact it can make on changing our lives for the better. People with trauma are typically struggling just to get through the day, focusing on managing their symptoms, and are often functioning in survival mode. Trauma clients I've worked with often have a difficult time even thinking about what they want beyond having their basic needs met, and maybe experiencing some peace and comfort in their bodies and their lives. The law of attraction can be a great catalyst for healing and moving out of survival mode.

The law of attraction is a universal law that states "that which is like unto itself is drawn," meaning that like attracts like. Our thoughts, beliefs, and actions consist of vibrations that attract the people, experiences, and situations into our lives. Negative thoughts, beliefs, and actions attract negative people, experiences, and situations, whereas positive thoughts, beliefs, and actions attract positive people, experiences, and situations. This can be hard to take in at first, and many people often think, "Why on earth would I create such a horrible experience for myself?" There's a famous quote by Gloria Steinem, the famous women's rights activist, that goes, "The truth will set you free. But first, it will really piss you off." Realizing that you have been creating your life by default and attracting negativity into your life can be overwhelming and difficult to accept. Knowing that you have everything within you to create the life of your dreams, however, is empowering. By using your newfound awareness along with your focused intentions, you can begin making changes in your life right away!

When working with the law of attraction, it's important to let go of a victim mentality and believing that other people have the power to influence what happens to you. Once you understand that it's your movie – you're the writer, director, producer, and star – and other people are just actors playing the parts you've given them, you can work toward creating the reality you've always dreamed of. Remember, everything is just a vibration. Beliefs are just thoughts you've thought over and over again until they became a belief. If you change the thought, you change the belief, which changes your vibration, which changes what you are attracting!

When I ask my clients what they want to create in their life, if I could sprinkle some fairy dust on them and have their life exactly the way they'd like it, they usually pause and have a difficult time picturing it, or it's a vague concept that they can't quite put their finger on. It seems strange doesn't it, that it's hard to know what we want? But the truth is, our primitive minds are programmed to focus on the negative for our safety and security. Our brains are wired to look for the negative (i.e., danger) as a protective measure in order to keep us safe from peril. This is especially true if you have experienced trauma. The brain is constantly on high alert, and the amygdala, the part of the brain that processes fear and memories, sends messages to the insula that contains plenty of negative emotions and very few positive ones.

People with trauma histories have a natural tendency toward negativity and negative emotions, so it's important to spend time building momentum toward positive thinking. You may have heard someone say that you've got to focus on five positive thoughts to counteract one negative one, or that you need to hold on to a positive thought for at least 17 seconds in order for it to create a new vibration in your body. This is because you've got to rewire the negativity and make the positive thought the new go-to vibration. It's like working out and strengthening your muscles, you're building your positive thought muscles. Doing the exercises in this chapter will help you strengthen your positive thinking muscles and build positive thought momentum.

The final component to successfully using the law of attraction in your life is intention. All goals, dreams, and desires begin with intention. We use intention by focusing in-depth on an end result or goal, and then making the commitment to taking the necessary steps to achieve it. Intention is continuous and consistent attention focused on the desired outcome. Wayne Dyer, in his book *The Power of Intention*, wrote that we should think of ourselves being surrounded by the conditions that we want to produce in our lives. In other words, we need to take time to imagine or visualize ourselves living the life as we intend it to be.

Our outer world reflects our inner world, so it's important to take time each day to make our inner speech and vibration align with our desires. We attract what we are and what we vibrate, so if we want to manifest a mate who is confident, compassionate, and loving but we lack confidence, are judgmental, and don't love ourselves, it will be pretty difficult to bring this person into our lives. The key is to get clear on what it is we truly desire, and then be willing to make the changes within ourselves to get in alignment with the desired outcome. By consistently doing daily practices to raise our vibration, we're able to attract more and more positive people and experiences into our lives.

Exercises for Raising Your Vibration

Make a list of your goals and intentions: This is a great exercise for getting clear on what you want to bring into your life. How to do it: Take some nice, deep relaxing breaths. Focus on your heart, and as you tune in to your heart, ask yourself what it is that your heart truly desires. Take as much time as you need, then begin to write out what you want to manifest in your life. Be as clear as possible in what you desire and get detailed on what that looks like to you. If you find you're struggling coming up with things, make a list of what you *don't* want. We don't always have to learn through negative experiences, but the great thing about contrast is that we can identify what we DO want by knowing what we DON'T want. By making a list of the things that you don't want, you'll be able to turn them into positive statements of what you do want. For example, "I don't want to be sick and tired anymore" can be turned into an intention with "I take excellent care of myself" or "I'm healthy, radiant, and full of energy."

Really put some time and thought into this. Here are some more tips on creating your list of goals and intentions:

Make them quantifiable – Don't just say "I want a lot of money" – write down dates you want to achieve it by, dollar amounts you want to earn, pounds you want to lose, qualities you're looking for in a friend or mate.

Write each statement in the positive – The universe doesn't recognize a negative. Instead of saying "I don't want to smoke anymore," you could say, "I'm tobacco-free and my lungs are clear and healthy."

Write each statement in the present tense – Saying "I will" keeps it out in the future. It may feel funny or awkward at first because you're saying something in the present tense that hasn't happened yet, but acting *as if* it has already manifested is very powerful.

Read your list twice a day – Read your statements out loud, once in the morning and once at night before bed. Consistency is key. Reading them out loud is great if you can because it makes it more powerful with the vibration of your voice.

Give it at least 30 days – It takes some to replace old negative thought patterns with the new positive ones, so stick with it for at least 30 days. You've probably had these thoughts and beliefs from when you were very young, and the neural pathways are deeply ingrained like six-lane highways in your brain. As you continue to read the list of your intentions daily, you'll be creating new neural networks and it takes time for those to settle in.

Edit or make any adjustments as needed – Sometimes we think we have a clear picture of what we want, but then realize it wasn't quite right. I tend to manifest things quickly and occasionally my desires change, or I need to teak something because it wasn't quite right. Do this if you need to and don't feel like you're locked into something because you wrote it down and have been reading it every day.

Once you've created the list of items that you want to manifest, it's important to check them against your belief systems to make sure that you're not unconsciously pushing them away. I really like this additional step when using the law of attraction and got this from Kim Beekman and her Inner Alignment program.

As you read each item on your list, ask yourself the following:

- Possibility – do I believe it's possible to achieve?

- Trust – do I trust that it will come to me?

- Worthiness – do I believe I'm worthy of it?

- Abundance – do I feel the abundance of it?

- Ease – does it feel easy to achieve?

- Detachment – am I detached from the outcome?

If you find that you feel stuck or uncertain in any of these areas, take a day for each belief and really try on each one as you think of your intentions. Start with "possibility" and go through the entire day thinking about your intentions becoming possible for you. Feel it, know it, and believe it to be true for you. Once you feel comfortable with that, move on to "trust" and go through the day with the same process as before, trusting that your desires are coming to you. Go through the rest of the beliefs in the same fashion.

Positive Thought Momentum: This exercise is a great way to begin shifting habitual negativity into positive thoughts. If you can hold positive thoughts for 68 seconds, it builds a positive thought momentum. Building up the momentum of each positive thought in sequence and holding the thought in your mind allows you to strengthen the neural pathways in your brain that are focused on the positive. How to do it: Begin by writing down four positive statements of things that you want to manifest in your life. The positive thoughts can be general or specific. Ideally, the statements are on the same goal or intention, and they build on one another in sequence. Repeat the first statement over again for 17 seconds, then move to the second statement and repeat it for 17 seconds and continue doing the same thing for the third and fourth statements. Once you finish all four statements, sit in the energy of the positive thought momentum for 3 minutes. For example, you could say, "I take excellent care of my body" and keep repeating it for 17 seconds, then you'd say "I am comfortable in my body" and repeat that for 17 seconds, then say "I love and appreciate my body for all that it does for me" and repeat for 17 seconds, and finally repeating "I am at peace with my body" for 17 seconds. Then hold on to the positive feeling of the vibration of those statements for 3 minutes.

Destination Vibration: I got this exercise from Kim Beekman in her Inner Alignment program. The destination vibration basically takes your list of goals and intentions and brings it to life in your mind and body and incorporates the senses and emotions, so that you're feeling, seeing, experiencing your life as if your intentions have already manifested. It's very powerful! How to do it: Sitting with your eyes closed, taking in some nice, deep and relaxing breaths, bring your goals and intentions to mind. Begin to visualize what your life would look like if everything has already manifested, and that you are living these manifestations right now. Imagine that you are sitting in a movie theater and your life with your fully manifested desires and intentions is playing up on the screen in front of you. Become aware of the feelings you're experiencing as you're observing yourself living your life as you fully intended. Fulfilling your dreams and desires, allowing these feelings and emotions to soak into your being, whether it's passion and excitement, joy, peace, and happiness. Allowing these feelings to flow through you and throughout your entire body, filling every cell with those positive vibrations of your fully manifested intentions. Feel into your heart and experience deep gratitude for the manifestation of your intentions, gratitude for living a life full of your heart's desires, and for your intentions having already manifested in your life.

The Violet Flame: This might seem a little strange to some people at first, but I've used it with hundreds of clients and it truly helps people clear negativity and raise their vibration. This was one of the first tools I learned when I began my spiritual journey in 2006, and I still use it daily. The great thing about the violet flame is that it is easy, quick, and efficient to use and you can do it from anywhere. It is made up of love (pink), wisdom (gold), and power (blue), and when these are combined, they create the violet flame. Violet is the highest vibrating color of transmutation, fire is the fastest form of transformation, and together they become an amazing way to transmute, transform, and transcend lower vibrating energies, thoughts, patterns, and beliefs. I work with people from all different types of backgrounds, religions, and beliefs, and there's one thing they all have in common: they all experienced tremendous shifts in their lives using the violet flame. It helps remove resistance, clear negativity, and elevate your vibration so that you can come into alignment with your intentions and desires. If you're feeling skeptical, or you have never heard of or worked with the violet flame, give it a try for a few weeks and see what type of shifts take place in your life. How to do it: Gently close your eyes and take in a few deep, relaxing breaths. Visualize a column of white light surrounding you, flowing infinitely up and infinitely down. Then picture the violet flame surrounding you, flowing through you and all around you. You can say aloud, "I call upon the violet flame to surround me now to clear my energy and raise my vibration." When you're ready, give yourself permission to let go of and release any lower vibrating energies, thoughts, patterns and beliefs, and send them into the violet flame to be transmuted and transformed. Continue releasing what is no longer serving you – any negativity, negative emotions, obstacles or blocks, lack or limitation, or anything else that has been keeping you stuck. Send it into the violet flame. If you have a specific intention for the violet flame, state it aloud. This could be something like "Please clear any fear and anxiety now," and then release it to the violet flame. You can end the process saying "Thank you. And so it is. Amen" or whatever feels right to you. Repeat as often as you need to!

Clearing and Balancing Chakras: Almost everyone these days has heard of chakras, the energy centers in the body that are responsible for the flow of life energy, also known as chi or prana. There are seven main chakras that are located along different points on the body, and they are connected to various organs and glands within the body. Each of the chakras carries a specific meaning, is associated with a color, and influences different areas of our life and health. Stress, lifestyle, negative thoughts, habits, or patterns can create a disturbance or block in the energy flow of chakras. When a chakra is disrupted or blocked, the life energy also gets blocked, and it creates issues in our lives on all levels – physical, emotional, mental, and spiritual. People who have experienced trauma often have disruptions or blocks in their chakras due to the negative effect that trauma has on their minds and bodies. Because of this, it's important to take time to clear and balance these energy centers in order to restore the natural flow of life energy. Here is an image describing the chakras in more detail:

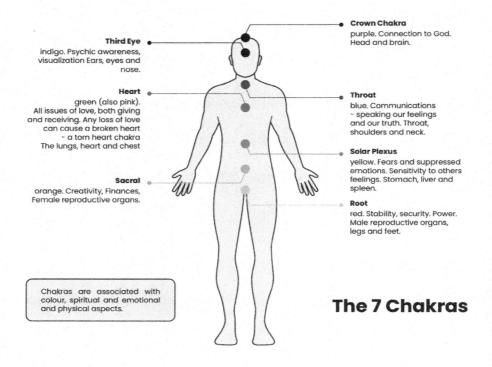

Crown Chakra
purple. Connection to God.
Head and brain.

Third Eye
indigo. Psychic awareness,
visualization Ears, eyes and
nose.

Heart
green (also pink).
All issues of love, both giving
and receiving. Any loss of love
can cause a broken heart
- a torn heart chakra
The lungs, heart and chest

Throat
blue. Communications
- speaking our feelings
and our truth. Throat,
shoulders and neck.

Solar Plexus
yellow. Fears and suppressed
emotions. Sensitivity to others
feelings. Stomach, liver and
spleen.

Sacral
orange. Creativity, Finances,
Female reproductive organs.

Root
red. Stability, security. Power.
Male reproductive organs,
legs and feet.

Chakras are associated with
colour, spiritual and emotional
and physical aspects.

The 7 Chakras

<u>How to do it:</u> Gently close your eyes and take in some deep, relaxing breaths. Bring your awareness to your root chakra. Notice if you're aware of any blocks or imbalances there, and if there are, visualize a ball of red light in the area of your root chakra slowly rotating clockwise. See it clear and bright and perfectly balanced. Next, focus your attention on your sacral chakra. Again, notice if there are any blocks or imbalances there and visualize a ball of orange light in this area, clear and bright and balanced. Continue working your way through each chakra clearing and balancing them as you go. When you are finished, visualize a column of white light surrounding

you, infinitely up and infinitely down, flowing through you and all around you. Practice this daily at first, until you feel like there are minimal blocks or disturbances, then just do this as needed when you are feeling imbalanced.

Chapter 10

Step 3 – Managing Your Thoughts

"The mind is not a vessel to be filled, but a fire to be kindled." – Plutarch

In 2008, on the floor of my living room, I began putting together a treadmill I had just purchased at the sporting goods store a few hours earlier. I was a single mom with a four-year-old daughter, and I worked full-time, which didn't leave a lot of time for exercise. Running had always been my go-to exercise, so I bought a treadmill with the intention of getting in some exercise in the mornings before my daughter woke up. During the assembly process, my nose started running and I got a sore throat, but I continued working on the treadmill. By the time I finished putting it together, I had come down with full-blown bronchitis! It was one of the strangest things I'd ever experienced.

For several years prior to this, I had an ongoing joke about how every time I would go out for a run, I would start to get sick, as if my brain was sending out a distress signal to my body saying, "Mayday! Mayday! We need to shut this girl down before she does this more often!" And sure enough, a couple of days after that run, I'd be down and out with bronchitis. During those years, the time between the run and getting sick got shorter and shorter, to the point where I could feel it kicking in within a few hours afterward. I could never quite figure out what was going on, and just thought I was run down or that my immune system had been weakened by stress or insufficient sleep. It wasn't until that night putting together the treadmill and getting bronchitis *before* I even stepped onto to it, that I realized there had to be something going on in my mind that was causing this.

I was already a couple of years along on my spiritual journey by that time, so I was pretty familiar with the mind-body connection. I was taking hypnotherapy courses and I was aware of how powerful the mind can be. During a regression therapy session after the treadmill incident, I discovered that I had an unconscious belief that I would literally die if I exercised, which had been unintentionally planted there by my therapist in the late 1990s during therapy for bulimia and over-exercising. The ongoing joke about my brain sending messages to my body that I was in danger was actually very close to the truth. I recalled my therapist telling me that I was killing myself running so much and purging, and my subconscious must have stored that away as a danger to me. I recovered from bulimia, so the purging wasn't a factor anymore, but I still enjoyed exercise and running was my favorite. In the regression session, I cleared the belief that running was dangerous and rewired my brain, creating new neural pathways with positive thoughts about running and exercise in general. That experience taught me how truly powerful and adaptive the mind is.

There's a famous quote by Anne Lamott that goes: "My mind is like a bad neighborhood. I try not to go there alone." If you have unresolved trauma issues, this can be particularly true, since the overactive amygdala in your brain remains on high alert, sending messages that everything is a danger and threat, and negative thoughts and memories repeat on a continuous loop in the mind. In my work with trauma clients, I've found that they tend to be overly critical and have a negative-focused mind toward themselves and others, as well as the world in general. I believe this is often because of a hypercritical parent or caretaker, and their inner critic has emerged as a predominant player to fill this role in their adult life. The amygdala also influences this by communicating with the insula, the area of the brain that associates with introspection and emotional awareness. When the overactive amygdala gets involved, it causes a profusion of negative emotions and very few positive ones.

We also have negative thought patterns and beliefs that are buried in our subconscious mind, which often wreak havoc in our lives, causing self-destructive behaviors and resistance to change. It's important to understand how we process and store information in order to move past some of the barriers, obstacles, and blocks that our minds create for us. The mind is made up of several levels of consciousness and each level influences our habits, beliefs, patterns, and behaviors.

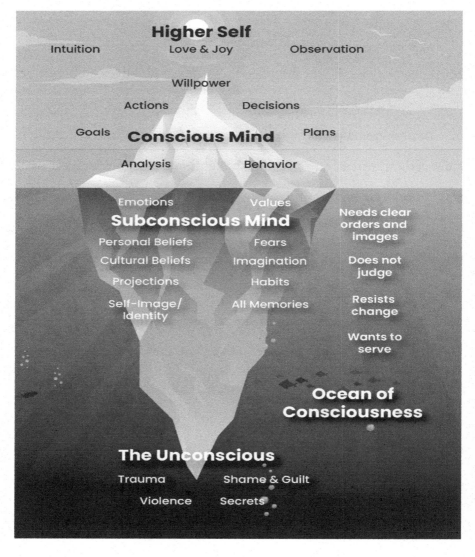

Unconscious: The unconscious mind is where hidden trauma, abuse, secrets, and shame are stored. This part of the mind keeps our traumas tucked away as a means of protection until we are ready to heal and process them. Many trauma survivors experience childhood amnesia or have difficulty remembering the events or details of them because it may have been too overwhelming or horrific, and they would not have been able to function or cope in everyday life.

After years of therapy and healing, something was said to me at dinner one evening and it was like a door was opened in my mind. I almost immediately began experiencing memories and flashbacks of events I had no memory of or had only vague recollections of the events. It was unpleasant and disconcerting, but I was at a place in my life where I could begin processing and healing. Unlike the subconscious where we can retrieve information and rewire for change and healing, the unconscious mind keeps things in lockdown until we are ready and able to deal with them.

Subconscious: The subconscious level of the mind is where our personal and cultural beliefs, projections, self-image and identity, fears, habits, thought patterns, and memories are. The subconscious works on your behalf to keep you safe and can be very resistant to change if the new goal or behavior is inconsistent with the underlying fears and beliefs. This is why we can consciously make a decision to change something in our life for the better but then quickly find ourselves right back in an old habit or pattern without even realizing what happened.

We form our beliefs about ourselves and our lives by the time we are six or seven years old. Imagine what our perspective was from that age, without a fully developed brain and unable to process information from a rational or logical point of view. We didn't have the ability during those early years to fully comprehend the world or how life worked. Our minds were programmed through a child's perspective, and neural pathways were created based on our experiences and interactions with our parents or primary caregivers, who also were programmed at an early age. We've been living our lives reacting to, and getting triggered from, these old thoughts, programs, and patterns, many of which possibly weren't even ours to being with.

The power of the subconscious mind should not be underestimated, as it processes 20,000,000 environmental stimuli per second compared to the 40 environmental stimuli per second that the conscious mind processes. That's 500,000 times faster than the conscious mind. It is a workhorse and is recording everything beyond our conscious awareness. It is working on your behalf and believes that it is keeping you safe and protecting you from danger. The downside is that it filters everything from the perspective of your childhood programming and experiences, so until you overcome and rewrite that programming, it may more likely be hindering your progress more than helping it.

Even though it may seem overwhelming, it is our responsibility as adults to heal and rewire the programming that is keeping us stuck in these negative thoughts, patterns, and habits. We now know that the mind has plasticity, the ability to create new neural pathways and overwrite the old negative ones. We have the ability to free ourselves from the negativity loops and tapes that play over and over in our minds, and replace them with positive ones that support us in our desire to live the life we choose, rather than living life by default and remaining a victim to old programming.

Conscious: The conscious mind makes up a small percentage of the four levels of consciousness. While the unconscious and subconscious together total around 95 percent of the mind, the conscious level comes in at just under 5 percent. This is where willpower, goals, actions, logic, analysis, and critical thinking are. It's not impossible to achieve something at the conscious level if the subconscious is not fully on board with it, it just takes a lot more grit, determination, and staying present through the process to make it happen.

Although the conscious level is one of the smallest parts utilized by the mind, it is where we want to create from. The conscious mind is awareness in the present moment, which is where the power of creation lies. We often make decisions or have knee-jerk reactions to triggers from our subconscious, which is connected to the past, causing us to repeatedly relive the pain in what seems like a never-ending cycle. When we bring our awareness to the present moment, we can create a future that is no longer tied to the old programming. We do this through mindfulness, raising our vibration, and reprogramming the old, negative thoughts and patterns.

Superconscious: The superconscious mind is also known as universal consciousness. It is unified, one mind, infinite, and a higher consciousness outside of self. It is thought that most people utilize or tap into the superconscious mind less than one percent of the time. Edgar Cayce, a well-known psychic known as the "sleeping prophet," gave readings in a trance-like state and diagnosed illnesses without ever studying the subject or meeting the individual. Many people believe that he accessed the superconscious while in his trance-like state and received the information needed from this infinite source of higher consciousness.

Spiritual and physical healing come from the superconscious level, and it is the location of intuition, peace, kindness, forgiveness, and love. The superconscious mind is the infinite intelligence that controls the universe and it's the collective consciousness of all existence. We can work on accessing the superconscious through a variety of practices such as meditation, yoga, stillness, prayer, mantra, and breathwork.

The mind is an amazing and wondrous part of the human experience. We use our minds to solve complex problems, create music and breathtaking works of art, and communicate with others through speaking, reading, and writing. Our subconscious minds run the automated systems in our bodies, beating our hearts, breathing for us, and detoxing foreign or dangerous substances. And yet, our minds can also be the source of incredible suffering, trapping us in our own personal hell, keeping us locked in a self-imposed prison created by our negative thoughts, patterns, and self-destructive behaviors. We get through each day, living a lonely, isolated existence in our heads, looking everywhere but inside ourselves for a way out and not realizing that we've been holding the key to our freedom all along. Once we realize that we're the ones keeping us stuck, we gain the power to set ourselves free.

There are three things that we must do in order to move forward on the path to freedom and finding that peaceful place within us. First, we need to cultivate self-awareness by observing and noticing the negative thoughts, patterns, beliefs, and fears as they present themselves in our lives. To do this, we need to be a detached observer, like a scientist watching an experiment unfold. I'll notice something I do or think and then say to myself, "Hmm, isn't that interesting how that person said something to me that I perceived as critical, and then I became upset and defensive trying to justify my worth to them. I wonder where that response is coming from and what is triggering it." By staying curious and just noticing what played out, I don't attach to it and I don't judge the person or my response. If I get attached or judge, I'll go into a flight response or my inner critic will want to get in on the action, and then I won't be able to identify the pattern or underlying belief. As you get the hang of this, you may start catching yourself mid-reaction and be able to adjust your response to the situation. After a while you might even notice after the fact that you responded in an entirely different way than you used to. That's rewiring your brain synapses and neural pathways in action!

Once you've been able to increase awareness of your negative thoughts, patterns, and behaviors, the next thing to do is move into a place of acceptance. I've found that this concept can trip people up sometimes and create a wall or barrier to healing. If this happens, just go back to noticing and observing it. When I notice this, I'll say something to myself like, "Isn't it interesting that I'd rather complain about this situation and wish it were different than the way it is, even though I know it can't be changed. I wonder why I want to stay stuck in this negativity instead of accepting it and moving on."

When I do this, something will come up showing me where the resistance is. For example, I may not want to accept it because I want my hurt or pain to be acknowledged, or I want an apology, or there's a belief that if I accept it and let it go I won't have anything to justify the pain and suffering I experienced.

When I acknowledge what's going on and sit with that for a bit, I'm usually able to release the resistance and move into acceptance. It may look something like this: "OK, so I'm still feeling frustrated and upset that my knee keeps flaring up even though I'm eating healthy and taking excellent care of myself. I know on a conscious level that my body is detoxing the inflammation and toxins from my autoimmune issues and that it takes time, but physical discomfort tends to be very triggering for me and I'm having difficulty accepting the situation. I don't want to eat to comfort myself or distract myself with unnecessary busyness because those were my old patterns and ways of coping, and I want to stay mindful and present despite the discomfort. What is it that I really need right now so I can create some peace within this issue?" And then I wait to see what comes up and I respond to it.

I found that once I stopped abandoning myself when I was triggered or in resistance and took the time to uncover what I really needed in that moment, the resistance melted away and I was able to move into acceptance. Occasionally, I still want to pitch a fit in my mind, so I honor that and then circle back to it when I'm ready. However, it doesn't take very long for me these days to decide that I want to get out of the lower vibration and into a more peaceful place as quickly as possible. This exercise has been invaluable for me and we'll go into it more in the forgiveness section, but I recommend practicing this as often as you can. When you can get to acceptance on just about anything, and I'm talking about everyday stuff, not only trauma or major issues, you free yourself from a whole lot of struggle and unnecessary suffering.

When we move into acceptance, we release resistance, which opens the flow of allowing positive people, events, and situations into our lives. Resistance is pushing against something that we fear or don't want. Imagine that you're trying to push a giant brick wall away from you. All of your energy is going into moving the brick wall, but it's not budging. You can't think of anything but that brick wall and how much you want it to move, and it's irritating you that it's there, even though you can't entirely remember why you don't like it in the first place. It's become such a habit that you can't think of a time when you weren't pushing against it, you just know that you don't like it so you keep pushing against it hoping it will eventually move.

If you're like me, you may throw a couple of curses at the universe and say, "Why did you put this brick wall here?! You know

I don't like brick walls, they're dangerous and scary and I don't feel comfortable with this wall being here." Usually I would get a whole lot of silence as a response, so then in frustration and anger, I would shake my fist at the heavens and cry out, "OK, fine, screw this wall. I'm exhausted and I just can't push against it anymore. I didn't ask for this stupid wall, I don't want there, but it doesn't seem to be going anywhere. I'm done. I give up." Then I would walk away (or crawl depending on how long and difficult my battle with the wall was), and then in the ultimate act of defiance, I would start doing something else, completely unrelated to the wall, like read a book or watch a movie. As soon as I settled into the new activity, my mind and body relaxed; it was like I could feel the loving response of the divine roll over me like a gentle wave, whispering softly to me, "Finally."

As many times as I've experienced this, the gift of surrendering and letting go never ceases to amaze me. As soon as I move into acceptance, it's as if the stars align and I get clearer on my purpose. I'm motivated and focused, and I'm riding the waves of flow and abundance. Once I get out of my own way, I begin allowing all the wonderful gifts and opportunities to come into my lie. Ralph Waldo Emerson wrote: "Most of the shadows of this life are caused by our standing in our own sunshine," and that couldn't be a more apt description of our experience with resistance versus allowing. Of course, it's not like we're intentionally doing this, our underlying fears and limiting beliefs are keeping us stuck in negative patterns and habits. Even if we're clear on our goals and dreams, if we're still pushing against the brick walls, we will be unable to manifest them into our lives. Or, we do manifest them in some form, but we aren't happy with what we created because they still have aspects of fear and resistance within them.

Resistance is any thought, belief, habit, or behavior, whether conscious or unconscious, that doesn't align with our desires. We can be crystal clear on our goals and dreams, doing positive affirmations, visualizing our future lives, and imagining our success. But if there's resistance (i.e., fear) about it, at the end of the day without exception, we will receive at whatever level we're vibrating. Resistance is based in the ego, is fueled by fear, and feels rigid and inflexible, closed-minded, and even irrational at times. It's often externally focused, based in trauma and unworthiness, and we tend to push away what we desire from the universe. We get edgy, irritable, and anxious that things aren't working out the way we wanted them to, which leads to anger and frustration. People in resistance will often go into judgment, becoming hypersensitive and overly critical, which can often circle back to victimization and shame, keeping them stuck in a cycle of triggering the trauma response over and over again.

Moving into acceptance releases the resistance and brings us into a place of allowing. When we're in a state of allowing, we're connected to the divine and our higher self, and in the flow of life. We're open to new ideas and concepts, our relationships are satisfying and loving, we feel more peaceful, and life becomes easy and enjoyable. When we're allowing, we're in our hearts. It's like floating peacefully on the water in a canoe and trusting that the river will take us wherever we need to go. We may experience some rapids or rough areas along the way, but we accept them and stay true to our course, knowing we're always loved, protected, and supported by the divine.

Resistance vs Allowing

Resistance	Allowing
Based in ego	Based in the divine
Externally focused	Internally focused
Judging and critical	In the heart, accepting
Rigid and inflexible	Flowing
Fear	Love
Distrusting	Trusting
Blocks and obstacles	Ease and effortless
Unworthiness	Worthiness
Energetic imbalance	Energetic balance
Closed-minded	Open-minded

5 Ways to Release Resistance:

1. *Increase Self-Awareness* – Become an observer to your negative beliefs, habits, thoughts, and patterns. Notice without judgment how you keep yourself blocked or stuck in certain situations or issues. Stay curious without attachment, like a scientist observing an experiment. Keep a journal and record beliefs and patterns that you notice you play out in your life. Having awareness of your thoughts and behaviors gives you the power to rewire and heal them.

2. *Stop Negativity in Its Tracks* – As you observe your thoughts and behaviors, especially the ones you want to change, you may notice a desire to shift the way you react. The first step to doing this is to shut it down as soon as you become aware of the negative thought, pattern, habit, or belief by stopping it mid-process. This is how you rewire the brain synapses and neural pathways in your brain. At first, it may feel like you're watching a train wreck happen that you can't stop or control, but with practice you'll find that it gets easier and eventually it becomes second nature. You can do this in a kind manner, firmly but gently. It's like being compassionate with yourself and at the same time setting a solid boundary for your inner critic. For example, if I have a pattern of negative inner talk about my

appearance and I look in the mirror and think, "Ugh, I look awful today. I shouldn't go out in public like this," I may shut it down by responding with "Thanks for sharing, but I don't think that way about myself anymore. I'm good enough just the way I am. I accept the way I look, now and always, end of story."

3. *Focus Your Attention Elsewhere* – Like in the example I shared earlier, as soon as I walked away and stopped pushing so hard against the thing I didn't want and started doing something else, the resistance shifted, and I moved into acceptance and allowing. It feels counterintuitive initially. We're taught to take action, to go out and make things happen. Surrendering and letting go of our attachment to the thing we're resisting feels strange or unproductive.

I've always been so goal-oriented and achievement-focused, accomplishing by doing and action. I took my spiritual growth and healing very seriously and there was rarely a time I wasn't reading, taking a course, or listening to a recording, entirely focused on healing and improving myself. So it felt like I was being extremely defiant when I stalked off and lay down to rest, took a bath, or read a book, because to me, that was the equivalent of throwing my hands in the air and giving up. It wasn't the most graceful approach, but I learned that it was exactly what I needed to do to let go of the resistance and shift into allowing.

When you find yourself struggling in resistance, focus your attention on something else. Find something to do that will distract you – perhaps it's time for self-care or enjoying a night out with friends. Getting out of your own way and letting go moves you into a place of allowing, where things flow easily and effortlessly.

4. *Let Go of Judgment* – I've found that people who have been on the spiritual or healing journey a long time tend to be hard on themselves when they encounter resistance or get stuck. They believe they should have "known better" or "done better," but they're still stuck, and they've made it worse by going into judgment and shame about it. We all get stuck. It happens. The key is being able to accept that's where you're at, and then willing to do what's needed to begin gaining some forward momentum again.

5. *Uncover What's Beneath the Resistance* – You've probably heard the saying, "What we resist, persists." Getting unstuck requires moving through the fear, and resistance is just a signal from your subconscious that you've gotten close to a sensitive issue; an underlying thought, pattern, or belief that's trying to

protect you from what it perceives as life-threatening danger. Try not to be too harsh with yourself when you experience resistance, it's just an indication to pay attention so that you can identify what's going on under the surface, and then you can move through it.

Exercises for Managing Your Thoughts

Mantras: Saying mantras is a great way to help with a busy mind, looping or obsessive/anxious thoughts, or when negativity hits. Looking at the root meaning of the word, *man* means "to think or thinker" and *tra* means "tool or instrument," so it basically translates into "a tool for the thinker." Mantras calm and center the mind and help relieve symptoms of anxiety, stress, and depression. A mantra is usually a Sanskrit word, phrase, or sound that is repeated in a mindful or meditative way, although I've seen them translated and said in English as well. Some people like to create their own mantras and say those too. I prefer the traditional Sanskrit mantras, as I believe there is a sacredness and higher vibration in the words and phrases when uttered in their original form that was created thousands of years ago.

Mantras are often repeated 108 times, which is a sacred number in Hinduism and yogic traditions. There are a couple of explanations for the significance of 108. First, the numbers 1, 0, and 8 represent one thing, nothing, and everything (infinity), and when the numbers are combined into 108, it represents the reality of the universe as being simultaneously one, emptiness, and infinite. Also, Vedic mathematicians calculated the distance between the Sun and the Moon to the Earth as 108 times their respective diameters.

How to do it: In a comfortable, seated position with your back tall and straight, begin the process of repeating a mantra of your choice. There are mantras for protection, abundance, peace, removing obstacles, and health. You can repeat your mantras to recordings and follow along, which is a great way to learn the pronunciation and flow of the words, or you can practice them silently in your head. Saying them out loud sends the vibration throughout your physical body, which adds healing benefits. Repeating them quietly in your head requires extra focus attention, which adds additional mindfulness benefits. You can also use mantras during activities such as walking, hiking, or driving, and they are still effective as long as they are practiced with love, awareness, and attention. I like to use mala beads when saying mantras. Malas, or prayer beads, are a string of 108 beads and are used for counting as you repeat each mantra. Many malas have dividers placed at the quarter and halfway marks along the string of beads that give you the option of doing a shorter number of mantras if time doesn't allow for the full 108 repetitions.

Guided Meditations: These are great to begin with because you can just sit or lie down while listening to someone else guiding you through the meditation, and it gives your mind something to focus on. Listening to someone else's voice in meditation, just like what would occur in a hypnotherapy session, provides a distraction for the conscious mind so that healing can take place under the surface in the subconscious mind. Guided meditations come in many different formats and cover a variety of topics from relaxation to healing to spiritual journeys. You may find as you try out different guided meditations that you like some people's voices, or music, or style better than others. I have a couple of dozen of my favorites and rotate what I listen to depending on my mood or needs at the time.

Observing Mind: A 2005 study by the National Science Foundation showed that we think an average of 60,000 thoughts per day and of those, 80 percent are negative and 95 percent are repetitive. There was also a direct correlation between quality of life and quality of our internal dialogue. My response when I read about that was "Whaaaat?!? That is CUH-RAAAZY! Who could possibly keep track of all those thoughts, much less shift them over to positive ones?"

Well, practicing an observer mind is a great place to start! It is a great technique to use if you have a hypercritical mind, chronic toxic shame, or perfectionistic tendencies. It allows you to step outside of the thought patterns of "not good enough" so that you can investigate where the belief originates from and challenge it in a compassionate way. It's like being a scientist and observing an experiment without your own bias getting involved. When we're curious about something, we can observe and ask questions without any negative attachment to the answers we receive. As you practice this, you'll find it becomes easier to challenge and rescript negative beliefs and patterns, until they no longer hold any charge or power over you.

How to do it: Begin by setting the intention that you want to develop awareness of your negative thought patterns and limiting beliefs. Start paying attention throughout the day as they crop up for you, and as you notice what is happening, shift into the observer/scientist mind. Be curious about the thoughts you're aware of and notice if there are any sensations anywhere in your body that are connected to the thoughts. You could observe aloud or in your head something like, "Well, isn't it interesting that I'm thinking about _____ and I'm experiencing _____ in my body." Or, "How interesting that I tend to _____ when I'm thinking about _____." To get to the belief underneath the thoughts, you can add, "Where is this thought coming from?" or "I wonder where the root of this thought pattern is" and wait for the response. It is helpful in the beginning to have a notebook or journal to record the observations, and then you can notice patterns or behaviors that are associated with the thoughts.

As you feel more comfortable observing without judgment and uncovering the belief, you can challenge it. Just by firmly stating something like, "Thanks for sharing, but that's not true and I don't believe that about myself anymore" or "That's an old tape playing and I choose to think only positive thoughts about myself now" or whatever feels right to you for the situation.

Re-scripting: This exercise expands on the observer mind technique by taking the thought pattern and underlying belief and changing the story. This is especially helpful for those who have experienced trauma, since they often get stuck in powerlessness because they were unable to or were prevented from taking action at the time of the trauma. Re-scripting works because the brain doesn't know the difference between what is imagined and what is real, so we can rewrite the story with actions that are empowering and provide closure.

How to do it: In a comfortable, seated position take in some calming and relaxing breaths. Gently close your eyes and focus your intention on the thought pattern and its underlying belief that you would like to rewrite. As you tune in to the negative or limiting belief, ask yourself where this belief may have come from. Allow yourself to remain open and curious as you receive the answer. Continue to gather more information such as whether this was your belief or was it taught to you, did it come down through your family, or was it created through an event or experience.

As you receive the answers, continue to stay in observer mind without judgment. If any memories come up while you're exploring the origin of the belief, allow yourself to remain unattached as you observe the memory. Now imagine changing the outcome of that memory ... perhaps you need to bring in another person to help, or maybe there are things you have to say that you weren't able to at the time. Take a few moments to play out the memory the way you want it to ... you are in charge. Good. Now think about what you needed and didn't get at that time. Was it a hug, some comfort or reassurance ... an acknowledgment or apology ... a friend or loved one to talk to so you could feel heard and supported? Take some time now to give yourself whatever you needed. Good. Once that feels complete, replace the old belief with a new positive statement. Repeat the positive statement several times and allow it to flow over your body like a warm blanket. When you feel ready, open your eyes and bring your awareness back to the room.

Gratitude: Most people understand that being grateful contributes to living a happier life, but gratitude can be a powerful tool for the mind because it can actually rewire the neural pathways in the brain and shift negative thoughts, beliefs, and patterns! It's literally impossible to complain and be grateful at the same time. Gratitude has been shown to reduce depression and anxiety, increase relationship satisfaction, and increase resilience in times of stress or difficult situations. When you practice gratitude, you raise your vibration and begin attracting *more* things to be grateful for. It's also a quick and easy exercise that you can practice in just a few minutes each day.

How to do it: There are a number of ways to incorporate gratitude into your daily routine. You can try them all or stick with whichever one you like, but be sure to consistently do them for at least 30 days.

Write a list of 10 things you are grateful for: One of the easiest ways is to write down a list of ten things you are grateful for each night and then read them aloud before you go to sleep. This allows you to bring a positive vibration and thought momentum in your dream state.

Three Good Things: A variation of the exercise above is to spend 5 to 10 minutes each evening writing down in detail three good things that happened to you that day, whether they were big or little, and describing why you think they happened.

Gratitude Visualization: Another gratitude practice you can do is to sit quietly in a comfortable position and think about what you are grateful for. Gently close your eyes and imagine the people, places, things, situations, and events that warm your heart, bring you joy, or that you greatly cherish. Sit in that feeling for 5 to 10 minutes. You can add an extra layer of gratitude by saying thank you for each of those things that you are grateful for in your life, and then allow that feeling to wash over you and flow through you and all around you. When you are ready, open your eyes and bring your awareness back to the room.

Write a Gratitude Letter: Spend some time composing a letter for something that you are grateful for. It can be to a person, but it doesn't have to be. I've written gratitude letters to the earth and the angels, and I even wrote one to my self-loathing when I decided it was time for us to go our separate ways. I've had clients write them to their bodies, their future selves, and to addictive substances. The possibilities are endless, just pick whatever you feel you need to express some gratitude for and start writing.

Chapter 11

Step 4 – Feeling Leads to Healing

"If you don't allow a feeling to begin, you also don't allow it to end."

– Geneen Roth

Being an empath and highly sensitive to everything around me, I've always been able to pick up on how other people were feeling. Even as a child I could sense people's moods and had an innate understanding that what they were saying didn't always align with what they were actually feeling or thinking. I also had a difficult time discerning between my own feelings and what I was sensing in others. I frequently had headaches and stomachaches and would use food to either soothe my discomfort or as a way to close off my empathic sensitivity. I was often criticized for being "too sensitive" and told that I needed thicker skin if I wanted to survive in this world.

When I began my spiritual journey and started studying energy healing, I learned ways to protect my energy and put up boundaries so I wouldn't take on my client's "stuff" as I worked with them. It took me years to master this and I'm still learning. Because of my deep desire to take away other people's pain, I would inadvertently process their issues through my own body, which often made me sick or exhausted. As I became more skilled in energy work, I began to notice that I could sense a client's physical or medical issues in my own body. I started scanning myself prior to sessions so I was clear on what was mine and what wasn't. I would also receive divine guidance regarding what the emotional or mental issues were that were creating the blocks and how to clear them.

Being empathic and highly sensitive can be both a blessing and a curse. Feeling the pain and heartbreak, rage, fears, and despair of others can be debilitating at times, especially if you don't have the tools to stay centered during the storm of other people's weather. However, being able to tune in to a client's energy and help them heal and release the past so they can feel love and joy again, is an incredible and humbling experience. Sensing divine love as it flows through me for another person, feeling my angels and divine helpers surrounding me, and the love, comfort, strength, and support that they provide to me on a daily basis is nothing short of miraculous. I used to hate being so sensitive, but I've learned to accept it and can now appreciate what a wonderful gift it truly is, despite the occasional discomfort and pain.

While I was going through my healing journey and visiting practitioners for various trauma healing sessions, one of them said to me, "You have to feel to heal, Allison," which at the time I thought was absurd because I literally feel *everything*! Another practitioner told me I needed to release my anger by hitting a pillow with a baseball bat and someone else suggested I take ice or glass and throw it against a wall outside for 15 minutes. I brushed off the advice because I didn't feel angry and I really just wanted to address the self-loathing, depression, and anxiety that was bringing me to my knees most days. I continued going to sessions and did some great healing work but still didn't acknowledge the underlying emotions that made me uncomfortable.

I later learned that what I had been doing from the beginning of my spiritual journey was called "spiritual bypassing," a process of using spiritual practices or tools to avoid facing unresolved trauma and difficult emotional issues. I stayed focused on love, light, and angels and kept myself busy helping others heal, which allowed me to avoid having to look at my shadow self, the dark stuff that made my skin crawl. It's like sprinkling flowers, rainbows, and sparkles on a big pile of poo. The poo is still there, and it still stinks. You just can't see it under the nice layer of pretty stuff.

I made a few unsuccessful attempts at processing feelings, still scared of doing much more than dipping my toe in the water of those deep, dark emotions. Feeling strong emotions such as anger or rage absolutely terrified me, like if I opened that door just a tiny bit, I would release the kraken and hellfire would rain down on the earth, incinerating everything in its path. The same went for feelings of self-loathing and despair, which inevitably led to thoughts of wanting to die, so it was necessary to keep a tight rein on those as well. Unfortunately, the unresolved emotional issues and trauma took a huge toll on my health and oozed out into my life in the form of anxiety, panic attacks, and treatment-resistant depression.

It wasn't until I experienced a retraumatizing incident a short while later that I finally became willing to deal with it head-on. During the incident, I was able to keep my eyes open and observe the dysfunction, the manipulation, the inability of the people to acknowledge their part or apologize for their actions, and the story they created about it to make it acceptable to them. For the first time, I was able to remain unattached as it unfolded, stand up for myself and not buy into their cruel words, or the threats that came when I refused to go along with their story. I was able to take care of myself and get to a safe place, and once I was settled and able to get centered again, I realized something else. I was angry. Furious. It was like I had been given a new pair of glasses and could see my life from a different perspective now. I saw clearly the lies, the manipulation, and the desperate desire I had to be loved and feel safe, that I was willing to accept the story and make it my reality too.

I couldn't unsee it though, and I didn't want to. But I also couldn't continue living with the anger and rage I was feeling either. I finally came to accept that there was no easy way around it and that the only way through was through. So I began a daily practice of feeling and releasing my emotions, and an amazing thing happened. Not only did my anxiety and depression symptoms dramatically decrease, but my chronic pain and inflammation did as well. I felt lighter and freer, as if a heavy, wet blanket had been lifted off of me. I became more grounded during stressful or challenging situations, and I was taking time to respond rather than react in triggering situations. I'm still highly sensitive and feel things very deeply, but I'm able to stay grounded and centered, and not get swept away by the tumultuous waves of emotions – whether mine or someone else's.

I tried half a dozen different techniques for feeling and processing emotions, and while I liked some of the processes, they didn't flow or feel quite right to me. So I ended up creating a process by taking a few of the techniques I liked and adding a few of my own. Some of the key components of the process that I found to be effective were incorporating mindful awareness, naming the emotion or feeling, feeling it in the body, acceptance, and reframing. Invoking mindful awareness or sacred presence creates a sense of safety and security, which is important when we may be dealing with some heavier emotions and feelings. Naming the emotion acknowledges it and brings our focus and attention to it, which is critical since we've most likely been avoiding doing just that for some time. Feeling it in the body and allowing yourself to sit with it provides the opportunity for it to come to the surface to be released. This is a key component since the end result is to release and let it go. As we know, trauma and emotions get stuck in the body, so it's important to allow the body time to process and heal.

Acceptance helps break down any walls or barriers to healing, such as denial, avoidance, or resistance. Using acceptance in this process helps us learn from the experience and begins the shift into the positive. Finally, reframing gives us the opportunity to change the story, especially if the emotion is connected to feeling powerless or the inability to take action at the time of the event or trauma. Reframing sets the stage for the final step of releasing and letting go of the emotion from your physical and mental bodies. I recommend using the "Feel and Heal" process as a daily practice, at least for a month or two and then switch over to doing it on an as-needed basis.

If you're like me, you might be tempted to skip this exercise with the intention of coming back to it later. The idea of intentionally feeling an emotion that in the past we may have gone to great lengths to avoid feeling can seem daunting or overwhelming. Once I started doing this though, I discovered two things: 1) I wasn't going to die from feeling a feeling even though I really thought I might, it's like the fear of feeling was worse than the actual feeling of it, and 2) I felt much better afterward. Every. Single. Time. It seems a little ridiculous now looking back, how much resistance I was in and the lengths I would go to in order to avoid doing this exercise. It's like going to the gym: I know it's good for me, but I drag my feet or make excuses. Once I get there and start working out, I remember how much I enjoy it and how great it feels to do it.

Here Is the Feel and Heal Process:

Begin by getting into a comfortable position, either seated or lying down. Take in some nice, deep relaxing breaths and follow the steps below.

1. *Invoke Mindful Awareness or Sacred Presence* – If you've been practicing mindfulness, take a moment to get centered and grounded, and shift your awareness to the present moment. You can also call in the divine or sacred presence (whatever that is for you) and surround yourself in a cocoon of divine white light and protection. Feel the white light flowing through you and all around you, feeling safe, secure, and protected.

2. *Identify the Feeling/Emotion* – As you sit for a few moments, become aware of what the feeling or emotion is that you are experiencing. You can say it out loud or in your head. If you are connecting to a feeling in your body such as exhaustion, hunger, or pain, what would this translate into if they were an emotion or feeling?

3. *Sense the Feeling/Emotion in Your Body* – Once you've identified what the feeling or emotion is, notice where you are experiencing it your body. Is it a knot in your belly, a tightness in your chest, a lump in your throat? Give yourself a few moments to become aware of where the feeling is in your body and just notice it without judgment.

4. *Sit with the Feeling/Emotion* – Take some time to sit with the feeling or emotion. Allow yourself to really feel it in your body. There may be some discomfort at first, but give yourself some time to allow it to come to the surface so it can be released and let go.

5. *Accept it* – Acknowledge the feeling or emotion you're experiencing. You might like to investigate a little further and ask what you can learn from it or how you can grow from the situation or experience.

6. *Reframe it* – Sometimes a memory comes up when we are processing emotions, particularly when we tune in to the sensations in the body. Because our bodies hold trauma and memories, they may come to the surface while we go through the process. Think about how you could rewrite or reframe the outcome. Was there something that needed to be said that you weren't allowed or able to say at the time? Was there something you needed in the situation, such as a supportive friend or someone there to help you? Did you need to take some type of action, like remove yourself from the situation or stand up for yourself? Take a few minutes to reframe the memory with what you needed at that time. Really feel the shift take place from feeling powerless or like a victim to feeling strong and fully supported and protected by the divine.

7. *Release it* – Now, with gratitude for the lesson and healing, take a few deep, calming breaths and allow yourself to release and let it go. Allow it to come to the surface, flowing out of your body and away from you, sending it into the violet flame to be transmuted and transformed. Or you can visualize it floating down a stream or river until it completely disappears. Take as much time as you need until the process feels complete.

8. Repeat if Needed – Sometimes when we go through this process, there are underlying emotions beneath the feeling or emotions we just released. If this happens, go back to step 1 and begin the process again so that you can release the underlying emotion as well. I've found that anger may be an initial emotion that covers up hurt or sadness, or that worry/anxiety may cover up fear or shame. As you continue to work through the Feel and Heal process, you'll notice it gets easier and more comfortable with consistent practice.

*Note: I use feelings and emotions interchangeably here to avoid confusion, although there are differences between the two. Feelings originate in the frontal lobe and are mental, affected by neurotransmitters and hormones. Emotions come from the limbic system, our primitive brain, and are more reactive and felt in the body. They affect and play off each other, and it can be difficult to discern the difference between the two.

Additional Exercises for Processing Feelings

Journal – Using a journal to write down your feelings is a great way to use self-care for the emotions. Journaling helps you track patterns or triggers so you can be prepared or resolve them more quickly. It has been shown to reduce stress, anxiety, and depression. A journal is also a great place for increasing self-awareness, clarifying thoughts and feelings, and improving problem-solving skills. Writing in a journal on a regular basis can improve the immune system and keep your memory sharp.

<u>How to do it:</u> Find a comfortable, quiet, and private space where you can take some time to record your thoughts, feelings, or experiences. You can use any kind of notebook or paper, nothing fancy is required for this exercise. I was resistant to journaling for years because I thought if I opened up to my feelings that I might not be able to switch them off. So, to motivate myself to begin the daily writing process, I bought some nice leather-bound journals and colorful pens. If you do not know what to start writing about, try beginning with writing about the events of your day. If you are struggling with self-esteem issues or depression, you can write down positive affirmations about yourself and your life or things you are grateful for. Here are some tips for beginning (or restarting) a daily journaling practice:

1. If you are concerned about getting too deep into your feelings, set a timer for a few minutes to start with and then see how things are going. If you are doing well, set the timer again for a few more minutes. If you are struggling and feel like you might get sucked under with too much emotion, shift your focus to positive affirmations or a gratitude list. Revisit the topic another time.

2. Write about challenging or triggering events in the third person.

151

3. Before beginning the journaling practice, imagine that you are surrounded by divine white light or a ball of pink divine love. Know that you are fully loved, supported, and protected as you go through this writing process.

4. If you are feeling stuck with what to write about, start writing your thoughts in the moment. That might even begin with *"I don't know what to write about but I know Allison said that journaling is supposed to be a great practice for self-care and so I'm giving it a shot even though I'm not quite sure what I think or feel about it right now."* It is OK to ramble on. Keep going without judgment or worrying about what is being written down. Pretty soon the words will begin flowing in a more confident and natural style for you.

5. Be honest. There is no need to worry about what people think or trying to look your best and appearing perfect on paper. This is just for you and your personal growth and development.

6. Write about your goals and dreams. Give yourself permission to think big and really go for it.

7. Journal daily. A consistent practice of writing down your thoughts and feelings has tremendously positive benefits

and can create huge shifts in your self-awareness, intuition, and overall emotional well-being.

Radical Acceptance – This is one of my favorite practices for emotional self-care. It completely changed the way I react to and deal with challenges, disappointments, and setbacks. Ruminating about situations or events that we cannot change or have no control over creates unnecessary suffering. Beating ourselves or others up over something that happened in the past perpetuates the cycle of pain. Radical acceptance helps with letting go and moving on and brings freedom and peace to your life. When we completely and totally accept something exactly the way it is right now, we are no longer giving it our energy or trying to control it. This process frees us from powerlessness and a victim mentality. We become empowered by radically accepting ourselves and our lives with a kind and compassionate heart.

How to do it: Find a comfortable and quiet space and begin by closing your eyes and taking in some deep, relaxing breaths. Imagine yourself surrounded by a bubble of divine white light, flowing through you and all around you. Feel safe, loved, and protected as you are being held in this divine light. Become aware of any areas of your life where you might be resisting or fighting reality. Some may be at the front of your mind and others may be a little less obvious. Consider situations or events you may be bitter or resentful about. Perhaps this is sometimes

153

thinking your life should not be this way, that if a situation changed or something went differently then you could be happy. Maybe you are frustrated or unhappy with life, and people often disappoint you. Think about ways you may try to control situations or behaviors of others or expect other people to change to make you happy. Good. Now that you have an awareness of areas you may be resisting, shift your focus to acceptance. Take some calm, relaxing breaths, breathing peace and calm into your heart. Say to yourself or out loud, "I am willing to accept." Notice any tension or tightness that you might be holding in your body and continue breathing peace and calm into your heart, sending it throughout your entire body. Continue saying to yourself or out loud, "I am willing to accept myself, my life, and these situations exactly as they are," until you feel your body relax and let go. When you are ready, bring your awareness back to the room and open your eyes. Repeat this practice as often as you need to.

Chapter 12

Step 5 – Moving Into the Heart

"There came a time when the risk to remain tight in the bud was more painful than the risk it took it took to blossom."

– Anais Nin

I stared across the room at him, unwilling to break eye contact or back down from the argument we were having. I hated confrontation and would go to great lengths to avoid it, taking on the role of peacemaker in most circumstances. But my husband had this uncanny ability to unearth all my deepest fears and hurts, the ones I wouldn't even look at or acknowledge within myself. Through his unintentional words or actions, he could summon all those deeply buried feelings of abandonment, betrayal, unworthiness, and not being good enough.

When this happened, it became my unconscious mission to make sure that he knew in no uncertain terms that he had hurt me and was usually accompanied by plenty of anger and verbal outrage. Then I would burst into tears because I wasn't actually mad, I was hurting, and I desperately needed him to see that he had caused my pain and for him to take responsibility for it. Of course, in the way that life lessons work, I rarely ever received an apology or acknowledgment of wrongdoing from anyone because that's the way my pattern plays out. I had to be the one to heal that within myself rather than relying on others to do it for me. They could certainly trigger it and bring it into my awareness, but it was up to me to do the actual inner work.

This time was different though and I didn't automatically go into my usual knee-jerk trigger response. As I stood there glaring at my husband in full battle-ready mode, I began to see things from a higher perspective. I saw that he wasn't doing or saying these things to intentionally hurt me, and it wasn't some diabolical plan of his to finally send me over the edge. I needed him to behave a certain way so that I could feel safe, but I realized that he wasn't acting out to purposefully cause me anxiety or distress. He was doing it because *he* was deeply hurting, and it was the only way he knew how to keep the demons at bay.

It only took about a second for all of this to play out in my awareness and become clear to me. Somehow, I had dropped into my heart and was viewing everything from a perspective of love and compassion. So, instead of lashing out with criticism or anger, which is how my trauma brain typically reacted in these situations, I did the opposite. I took in a calming breath and said to him, "It looks like you're going through a hard time right now and I want to be here for you. What can I do to help?" It wasn't at all the response that either of us expected, and it completed shifted the way we interacted with each other. It was like it rewired the reactivity process in our brains.

We still triggered each other and had disagreements, but we didn't repeat the automated trauma responses of the pattern anymore. We had been given some grace, the ability to pause in the moment, and choose love over fear. It wasn't always perfect or pretty, it was bumbling at times, but we learned to communicate in a way that allowed the other person to feel safe and heard. It's amazing what can be accomplished and how much can heal and shift when you're not always prepared and ready to go into battle all the time.

Dropping into our hearts and responding from a place of love is not a natural way to respond for most people. We've been taught by family members and traumatic events that being vulnerable is not safe and it's best to avoid it all costs. We've learned that vulnerability is a sign of weakness and people will hurt and take advantage of us in this state. We're taught to believe that it's better to appear to be strong and independent than to allow anyone a peek underneath the armor. We know the truth though, and maintaining this facade creates a dissonance between what we show to the world and our true selves. We crave connection, intimacy, and being seen for who we really are, but keeping others at a safe distance keeps us isolated, disconnected, and lonely.

The only way to bridge the gap and reconnect with our authenticity is to live in our hearts, take off the armor, and allow ourselves to be seen. In other words, learning to accept the discomfort of vulnerability so that you can live a more joyful and happier life. In her Ted talk on vulnerability, Brené Brown explains how shame leads to disconnection, but that vulnerability can negate feelings of shame. She found that people who lived wholehearted lives, who had a deep sense of worthiness, love, and belonging, fully embraced being vulnerable. She says that we live in a vulnerable world and we tend to numb ourselves rather than face it. And according to Brené, we can't selectively numb emotion, so when we numb vulnerability, we also numb joy and happiness. When we are willing to lean into the discomfort, we find that it monumentally changes the way we live and love.

Living a life from the heart takes courage to keep moving forward despite some discomfort, willingness to remain open to life, and commitment to keep coming back to the heart when your mind wants to run the show. It's not about perfection, it's about choice. Making the choice each day about living in your head or your heart, staying present or giving in to distraction, and presenting your inauthentic or your true self. Making those choices and trusting your heart gets easier with practice. The heart is an intuitive and intelligent organ and it sends more information to your brain than the other way around. The heart is your own internal GPS system, guiding you to your truth and authenticity. By tapping into the wisdom of your heart, you discover a limitless stream of love, inner wisdom, and compassion for yourself and others.

In the true paradoxical fashion, it's when we allow the walls and barriers that we've constructed around our hearts to fall away that we experience real love and discover our true selves. We put those walls up to guard against heartbreak and pain, but they also prevent us from accessing the infinite well within of divine love, power, and truth. When we make the decision to live from the heart, we give ourselves permission to drop the shield and become vulnerable. As we do this, we find that we were never more protected, safe, and loved than we are when living in the heart. Only love is real, everything else is an illusion, a false story we tell ourselves. As the introduction to *A Course in Miracles* explains, "Nothing real can be threatened. Nothing unreal exists. Herein lies the peace of God."

The heart is the center of our existence and we know this intuitively. When we talk about ourselves, we touch or point to our heart. In 1991 scientists discovered that every human heart has approximately 40,000 cells that create a neural network within the heart. These cells think independently of the brain, and they feel and remember things differently than the brain does. When we go about healing trauma or painful experiences, we can't approach it from the perspective of healing the brain alone. As we know from previous chapters in this book, trauma is stored in the body and our cells have memories of the trauma, which must be released from the body in order to heal. The same goes for the heart – its neural network is separate from the brain and must be healed and rewired as well.

We have an energy field around us that is about five to eight feet in diameter, which can now be measured by science. The heart has the strongest electrical field, stronger than the brain. Our hearts receive input from the field and send signals to our brains on what type of energy to send to the body. Gregg Braden, in his book *Resilience from the Heart: The Power to Thrive in Life's Extremes*, describes this phenomenon as heart intelligence. He describes cells in the heart called sensory neurites that influence our ability to create personal resilience. Developing a powerful heart-brain connection with the help of these sensory neurites allows us to access our intuition and subconscious, providing a pathway for healing and the ability to thrive during challenging times.

There's a popular saying: "When we heal ourselves, we heal the world around us," which can certainly be applied to living a wholehearted life. We have the power to change the energy in our fields by shifting the output in the electrical magnetic fields created by our hearts. When we begin rewiring our thoughts and shifting our beliefs, practicing gratitude, compassion, forgiveness, prayers, and mantras, we change the field of energy surrounding us. This has a positive effect on us because we begin attracting more and more positive and heart-based experiences into our lives. However, it also has a direct impact on our friends and loved ones and those we come across as we go about our daily lives.

When our energy fields contain the vibration of our heart-based living, other people pick up on this as they can sense it through their own hearts and fields. It is communicated through our energy fields on a subconscious level. The cells in their hearts receive the signals of wholeheartedness being projected through electrical magnetic waves being sent out from our hearts. Their hearts will begin to adjust the current signals being sent to their brains and energy fields and start aligning with the new vibration of our heart-based energy fields. We are hardwired to perceive the energy fields of others for survival purposes, but what a wonderful discovery to learn that we can have a positive effect on other people when we consistently live from the heart.

The heart is about 100,000 times stronger electrically and up to 5,000 times stronger magnetically than the brain. More information is sent to the brain from the heart than the other way around.

6 Ways to Live From the Heart:

1. *Resist the Urge* – Forgo the urge to numb, distract, or avoid discomfort. Most people hate discomfort and will go to great lengths to avoid experiencing it. We often turn to substances such as food, alcohol, caffeine, nicotine, or drugs to numb and soothe our nervous systems. We distract ourselves by binge-watching TV, scrolling on our phones, working too much, surfing the Internet, and endless to-do lists. If you can resist the urge for just a few minutes and give yourself a minute to sit with the discomfort, it might go away. If it doesn't, you can do the Feel and Heal process to find the underlying emotion connected to the discomfort and release it. According to Brené Brown, people who live wholeheartedly face discomfort head-on and embrace vulnerability because they know this keeps them in their heart, from which they live happier and more joyful lives.

2. *Use Words Wisely* – Be conscious and vigilant about how you talk about yourself and others. Words carry a vibration that is felt in the body and energy field and can impact our health and mindset. Living from the heart means being authentic and speaking your truth, even if it isn't always what people like to hear. Setting healthy boundaries or saying "no" to others can be challenging at first, but it's preferable to saying "yes" to something out of obligation and then feeling resentful because you didn't honor your own needs. You can be firm and strong when speaking to others, while being kind and loving at the same time. Use your words to lift up, inspire, and motivate yourself and others. If you're having an off day, honor that and give yourself some space by avoiding criticism or negativity.

3. *Take a Risk* – Wholehearted living means feeling vulnerable and exposed sometimes. This can feel scary initially since most of us have built our lives around playing it safe to avoid getting hurt. Start small at first if you need to. Ask someone for assistance rather than doing everything yourself because you don't want to owe anyone anything. Or do something for someone else without expecting anything in return. Be the first one to say "I love you." Love someone deeply without any expectation of those feelings being reciprocated. Apologize or

admit wrongdoing if that's out of your comfort zone. Taking a risk may feel uncomfortable temporarily, but the rewards are so worth it. Being vulnerable leads to a happier, authentic, and joy-filled life.

4. **Focus on Small Things** – It's admirable to want to make a huge impact on the world, but the truth is that the little things we do each day make a big difference in people's lives. My first healing business in 2008 was called Loving Hearts Healing Center and the tagline was "Healing the world, one heart at a time." I really had this vision of saving the world and healing everyone's pain and heartbreak. Over the years, as I opened and closed a few healing businesses, either due to financial or health reasons, I felt like a failure for not achieving my goal. But the reality was that I did help people during individual and group sessions, and in the classes I taught, my students went on to help others. The point is, we can make a big difference in small ways, so do what you can *now*.

5. **Change How You Evaluate** – We are taught to measure success by how much we make, how many homes or toys we own, the title on our business cards, how thin we are or the types of clothes we wear, and how many degrees we have. None of those things are bad, but we often compare ourselves to others and

find that we are lacking in one area or another. This just leads to feelings of shame and unworthiness, which is not where we want to be in wholehearted living. Change your focus to how you live and love, and make that the most important factor of success. Making living from the heart a priority in your life will improve your relationships, how you parent, your work life, and how you take care of yourself.

6. *Show Up* – This one is so important. I've found that when we are feeling disconnected, depressed, or overwhelmed, we tend to isolate ourselves. We cancel plans or quit making them, avoid talking to people, and have a hard time getting to appointments or commitments, even if we know they'd be good for us. We just want to curl up under the covers and watch TV, read a book, or go to sleep. Giving in to this temptation, though, keeps us stuck and perpetuates the pattern. I've found in my healing work and trauma healing program that people have a hard time showing up for themselves. When I finally made a commitment to myself and my own trauma healing, I promised to show up and that was a game-changer for me. If I didn't feel like going to work, a therapy appointment, or social commitment, I went anyway. If I resisted self-care practices, I did them anyway. Sometimes it sucked and it wasn't always graceful, but I learned to show

up for me and follow through on commitments. Showing up, being present and in your heart is truly one of the greatest ways to live from the heart.

Exercises for Moving Into the Heart:

Heart Mantras – We reviewed the benefits of mantras in chapter 10: Managing Your Thoughts, and in this section, we are using heart mantras to help shift the energy in your field into heart-based energy. Traditionally, it's best to say the mantra 108 times for the full benefit, but you can always do 27 or 54 times if time is an issue. *Mantra to Open Sacred Heart*: This mantra is best for melting into the sacred heart. "Hrim Shrim Klim Param Eshwari Swaha" [pronounced Hreem Shreem Kleem Par-um Esh-war-ee Swa-ha]. *Protection Mantra:* This is the perfect mantra if other people's energies have crowded into your field, if you're consumed by others' judgments of you, or you feel you are under psychic attack. "Om Eim Hrim Klim Chamudayei Vicce Namaha" [pronounced Om I'm Hreem Kleem Cha-Moon-Die-Yay Vichay Na-ma-ha]. *Mantra of Divine Love:* This mantra is believed to create pure love so the individual experiences his or her fundamental nature as one with divine love. Chanting Aham Prema affirms that the Self is pure divine love. "Aham Prema" [pronounced Ah Haum Pray-Ma].

How to do it: In a comfortable, seated position with your back tall and straight, begin the process of repeating a heart mantra of your choice.

166

You can repeat your mantras to recordings and follow along, which is a great way to learn the pronunciation and flow of the words, or you can practice them silently in your head. You can also use mala beads when saying mantras. Malas, or prayer beads, are a string of 108 beads and are used for counting as you repeat each mantra. Many malas have dividers placed at the quarter and halfway marks along the string of beads that give you the option of doing a shorter number of mantras if time doesn't allow for the full 108 repetitions.

Healing Heart Meditation – This is a great exercise for learning how to drop down into your heart. You'll become aware of what it feels like to be in the energy of the heart, and the wonders that you can tap into while you are there. This is where divine power, love, and wisdom reside and where you can access deep levels of your intuition and subconscious. Being present in this sacred space is what it truly means to live from the heart. <u>How to do it:</u> Sitting with your eyes closed, taking in some nice, deep, and relaxing breaths, gently place both hands over your heart. Begin to feel a warm, comfortable, and loving light in your hands and as this light grows, feel it spreading into your heart. Allow it to flow into your heart space and fill your chest area, bringing a sense of peace and calm and healing to your entire body. Ask your heart what it needs to hear right now to feel love and acceptance. Listen for the answer and then say the words to your heart, either out loud or in your mind. Feel your heart accepting the kindness and love, then send it throughout your entire body. Imagine a pink light flowing through you and all around you, and this pure divine love filling every cell of your body. As this pink light is flowing through you, notice how lovely it is to feel so loved and connected in this moment. Sit with this for a few moments as you allow this feeling to settle in. When you are ready, give thanks to your heart and the divine, and open your eyes.

Gratitude – Most people understand that being grateful contributes to living a happier life, and gratitude can be a powerful tool for the heart because it can actually heal and shift the electric magnetic pulses sent into the energy field by our hearts. The heart feels and experiences things differently than the brain, so practicing gratitude heals and rewires the neural network in our hearts. Gratitude has been shown to reduce depression and anxiety, increase relationship satisfaction, and increase resilience in times of stress or difficult situations. When you practice gratitude, you raise your vibration and begin attracting *more* things to be grateful for. It's also a quick and easy exercise that you can do in just a few minutes each day. <u>How to do it:</u> Follow the exercises described on pages 149–150 in chapter 10: Managing Your Thoughts.

Ask Your Heart – Your heart will never steer you wrong. This is where the source of divine power, wisdom, and love reside within you. In times of stress, chaos, or uncertainty you can always trust your heart to guide you in the right direction! In times of stress, the mind can get caught up in overthinking, analyzing, and worrying and will provide guidance that is based in fear or through the filters of trauma. The heart is always strong and true to what is in your best interests and highest good based in love. You can tune in to the heart and ask for guidance any time you need to. <u>How to do it:</u> Place your hands on your chest over your heart and gently close your eyes. Take in some nice deep, relaxing, and calming breaths. Tune in to the energy of your heart and visualize a pink light surround your heart. Allow this pink light to expand, flowing through you and all around you, until the pink light is completely surrounding you. As you inhale, breathe in pink light into your heart, and exhale it out into your energy field. When you feel centered in the sacred space of the heart, ask your heart a clear, direct question (or questions). Wait for the answer to come. Take all the time you need here. Once you feel you received the guidance from your heart, move your hands into prayer position at your heart and thank your heart for the love, guidance, and wisdom it shared with you. Slowly bring your awareness back into your body and back to the room.

Chapter 13

Step 6 – Forgiveness and Letting Go

"Forgiveness is not always easy. At times, it feels more painful than the wound we suffered, to forgive the one that inflicted it. And yet, there is no peace without forgiveness."

– Marianne Williamson

A few months ago, someone who I hadn't seen in a while told me I looked great and asked me if I had lost weight. At the time, I didn't think anything about it and although my weight hadn't really changed, I appreciated the compliment. Later that week, though, I realized what it was. I *felt* lighter. Like a huge weight had been lifted off me. My mood was light, as if the black cloud that seemed to always be hovering over me had disappeared. My heart felt full of gratitude for life, and I was silly and playful with others for the first time in years. Not the

171

fleeting good mood I occasionally experienced or the attempts at humor I often used to cover up my jaded and weary view of life.

No ... this was different. I was happy. Joyful actually. I was so unfamiliar with this feeling that I tiptoed around it for weeks, just waiting to see what would happen and not wanting to jinx it. It started out gradually, then grew into an intense joy that wanted to burst out of me like when you have good news you want to share with someone but have to wait for the right time and it becomes difficult to hold it in. After this feeling settled in a bit better, I took some time to contemplate what I was experiencing. Over the past few decades, I had become an expert on the hard stuff – depression, anxiety, trauma, pain, heaviness, shame, loss and so much more – and my focus had primarily been on how to just get through the day. I was definitely in unfamiliar territory here and needed guidance. As I reflected on my joyful state (and yes, it sounds ridiculous even as I type this because honestly, who has to question and wonder why they are happy?), the message I received was that I was finally learning to forgive and let go. Huh, interesting.

Before my spiritual journey began in the early 2000s, I really thought I was someone who forgave easily and moved on. I gave the people in my life multiple chances to learn from their mistakes and do better next time. I believed them when they told me they were sorry, and then ended up disappointed when they hurt me again. It was a frustrating process and somewhere along the way I became angry and resentful. I felt like a victim and powerless over the amount of energy I invested in being upset.

When I started to get sick in 2010, I knew I needed to do something to release and let go of the anger because it was really impacting my health. I read all the books I could find on forgiveness, did the worksheets and exercises in the books, and listened to many recordings on the topic. As I worked through the process of forgiveness, I felt shifts take place in some of my relationships, and I noticed that certain things people said no longer triggered me, so that was great. However, my body was still holding a lot and I continued to get sicker. I knew that for whatever reason there was a part of me that was unwilling to let go. It was like I needed to keep track of all the hurt so I could justify what happened to me and why I was so miserable. In my mind, I saw the hurts as a bucketful of tacks that people had stuck into me, and every time I tried to empty the bucket and let go, it would fill back up again. I wasn't ready or able to let go yet.

Most people misunderstand the concept of forgiveness. We think that if we forgive and let go, that we somehow condone or approve of the actions of others. Or we take the "holier than thou" approach and think when we forgive someone that we are somehow better than them because they are the ones who messed up and we have decided to gift them with our forgiveness. We might also forgive someone out of a sense of obligation because it's what we're taught or it's the spiritual thing to do. Finally, there is the illusion of forgiveness by pretending we are not angry or upset, or by making excuses for someone like "they didn't know better" or "they did the best they could."

What Forgiveness is NOT:
1. Forgiving by pretending we are not upset or angry
2. By forgiving someone, we condone their actions or behaviors
3. "Bestowing" forgiveness on someone
4. Forgiving by making excuses for someone's actions or behaviors
5. Forgiving because it is the right thing to do

These versions of forgiveness are not authentic and do not provide any real sense of relief from the pain, hurt, or anger we experienced from the event or situation. We must commit to the process of truly forgiving and letting go or it will just continue to cause suffering for us. Buddha said, "Holding on to anger is like drinking poison and hoping the other person dies." This is what it is like to continue to hold on to our unhealthy anger and resentment – we are the only ones who suffer, the other person has most likely moved on and forgotten all about it.

Think about how much time and energy you have spent being angry at someone or resenting them for their action or behavior. They might not even be in your life anymore. Years may have passed. For me, it was decades that I held on to some of my grudges. That takes a huge toll on us on all levels – emotionally, mentally, physically, and spiritually. Lack of forgiveness can affect many different areas of our lives. Whether we are aware of it or not, we bring the anger and bitterness into our new relationships and experiences. This affects our ability to trust others, be in the present moment with them, and open our hearts to fully love. We hold back a large part of ourselves to avoid getting hurt again, but the price we pay is that we are not able to experience the love and beauty of fulfilling relationships. This continues to perpetuate the cycle of anger and resentment, disconnection, and disappointment. We must begin the process of forgiveness in order to let go of the past, move forward in our lives, and experience peace within.

So what does it look like to truly forgive and let go? Just like with healing grief or loss, the process and timeline can be different for everyone. Some people are able to process their feelings and let go more easily, while others may take longer to get there. Of course, the amount of hurt and anger we are holding relates directly to the act committed, so the time needed to heal varies by our perception of the experience. One thing I found challenging was forgiving someone and letting go when I never received acknowledgment or an apology for what happened. I thought I really needed that because otherwise I just stayed stuck in the justification of my anger and resentments.

What I found when dealing with narcissists and their gaslighting behaviors, is that it can be difficult to forgive because they will usually change the story in order to not have to take responsibility for their actions and they often blame the victim. This can be very damaging psychologically, and I frequently questioned my sanity and whether the event actually did occur the way I experienced it. This is particularly true for those individuals who experienced ongoing childhood trauma or romantic partnerships with narcissists and domestic abuse – either verbal, emotional, or physical. Sometimes it feels easier to buy into the story and go along with it than to fight it because it is a battle that cannot be won, at least not one on one with them. The only way to "win" is to trust your gut, stay true to yourself, and do everything you can to forgive and let go despite knowing that you will most likely never receive that apology or acknowledgment for what happened.

Sometimes we are not ready and able to forgive just yet, and that is OK. There is a lot of guilt and shame that comes with not being able to forgive. We feel like we *should* let go and move on, so what is wrong with us that we are not able to? It is important to accept wherever you are at in the process, and trust that when the time is right it will happen for you. I have found when working with clients on forgiveness that it can be challenging to forgive people who have passed away. Even when someone is gone physically from our lives, we can still be holding on to anger and resentment for their actions while they were here. We may feel it is too late because they are gone. We might also carry guilt about their passing or for being upset and angry even though they are no longer here. It is important to forgive anyone in our life who has caused us pain – regardless if they are alive or not. If we are continuing to give our energy and power to it, then we need to work on forgiving and letting go. Again, moving forward in the process only when it feels right to do so. Forcing forgiveness will only end up in more feelings of anger, disappointment, guilt, or shame. Forgiveness is a completely personal process and there is no right or wrong way to how and when it is done.

Once we recognize our desire to move forward with the process, we find that there are tremendous benefits in forgiving. Forgiveness is one of the most effective ways to heal deep wounds. Studies have shown that the practice of forgiveness has positive psychological benefits for the one who forgives. Forgiveness has been linked to a decrease in depression, anxiety, unhealthy anger, and symptoms of PTSD. Forgiving others increases our empathy, compassion, and understanding. It releases the powerlessness of victimhood and we become empowered to take charge of our lives once again. The process of forgiveness allows us to no longer define ourselves or our lives by what happened to us or what other people have done to hurt us.

One of my teachers told me, "Forgiveness is loving yourself enough to take your power back." It truly has nothing to do with the other person, it is all about us. In a nutshell, forgiveness is *releasing ourselves from the burden of ongoing bitterness and resentment and freeing our hearts and energy to live life on our own terms*. By forgiving those who have hurt us, we are essentially clearing the way so we can finally experience the joy and beauty of living with improved health, mental clarity, passion, purpose, and peace of mind.

Benefits of Forgiving:

- Healthier relationships
- Improved mental health
- Less anxiety, stress, and hostility
- Lower blood pressure
- Fewer symptoms of depression
- A stronger immune system
- Improved heart health
- Improved self-esteem
- Setting better boundaries for yourself and others
- Increase in understanding, compassion, and empathy
- Increase in kindness toward self
- Fewer triggers and knee-jerk reactions

Self-forgiveness is another element of forgiving and letting go that we need to embrace in order to be able to move on and live happy, healthy, and joyful lives. Forgiving ourselves is just as important as forgiving others, possibly more so. Self-forgiveness can be challenging and tricky to navigate for several reasons. First, when growing up with narcissistic, abusive, or neglectful parents, children are conditioned to believe that everything is their fault. When painful things happened, they most likely took the blame or assigned it to themselves believing they deserved it. These individuals end up carrying the weight of responsibility for actions that are not theirs, and the guilt and shame of this burden can take a heavy toll on their health, emotions, and mental health. Learning to forgive oneself is especially important for these folks and they need to place the blame where it really belongs – on the individual or individuals who caused the pain. Not as a victim, of course, but to relieve the heaviness of a burden that is not theirs.

Another reason self-forgiveness can be difficult to practice is when individuals take on the role of keeping the peace in the family, or they dislike conflict and try to avoid it at all costs. In these cases, they are usually quick to let others off the hook or they make excuses for the behaviors and actions of others to avoid confrontation or unpleasant conversations. They tend to deny that they are angry or upset and often stuff down their feelings. Eventually though, the emotions find their way out – often in the form of harsh judgment and criticism of others or in a burst of rage or anger over something that tips them over the edge. When their emotions come out like this, they most likely feel guilt and shame about it, which just perpetuates the belief in being the peacemaker, avoiding confrontation, and feeling deserving of the painful behaviors of others. It is important for these individuals to acknowledge and accept their feelings, hold others accountable for their actions and behaviors, and set better boundaries for themselves and others. They can then begin the process of practicing self-forgiveness.

Finally, self-forgiveness can be challenging because many of us hold ourselves to a higher standard than we do of others. When we live our lives from a place of not feeling good enough, we tend to have high expectations of ourselves that can often be unrealistic and unattainable. We drive ourselves to exhaustion attempting to achieve that elusive perfection or by checking items off never-ending to-do lists to justify our existence. We are quick to let others off the hook, giving them the benefit of the doubt that they are doing the best they can. But when it comes to our own mistakes or imperfections, we berate ourselves for not doing better or knowing better and feel undeserving of love or forgiveness. In order to live a life with any sort of happiness or peace in it, we must begin to forgive ourselves and honor our imperfect humanness. Let go of the self-punishment and move toward self-compassion. Start by softening your heart toward yourself and know that you are inherently worthy of love and compassion.

The exercises I have included in this chapter are the ones that provided the biggest shifts and transformations for me. Some of these may resonate with you and some may not, so just choose which ones you are comfortable with and do those now. You can always revisit the other ones at another time. I found that there were days where I would do a few here and there as a part of my morning practices, and then there were times when I was doing them daily, several times a day like it was my full-time job. I highly recommend picking one or two that you can practice daily. Being consistent with this, even if it feels reluctant or awkward, truly provides the best results.

Exercises for Forgiveness:

Forgiveness Prayers – Prayers of forgiveness are an excellent and simple way to shift the energy of the situation and take your power back. There are many different types of forgiveness prayers, so I have only included a few of my favorites here, but feel free to explore other types that work for you.

Ho'oponopono – This is a powerful ancient Hawaiian forgiveness process. The Hawaiian word *ho'oponopono* comes from *ho'o* (to make) and *pono* (right). The repetition of the word pono means "doubly right"" or being right with both self and others. This forgiveness process allows you to disconnect the discordant energy between you and others in a positive, loving way. There are four steps to the practice – repentance, forgiveness, gratitude, and love. It is such a simple yet powerful tool to use for healing past hurts and letting go of the pain so you can move forward in your life. How to do it: Get into a comfortable position in a quiet space. Light a candle and play some soft instrumental music if you wish. Think of the person, event, or situation that you would like to forgive and heal. If you are not ready to forgive someone just yet, you can keep it general or use it for self-forgiveness. It is more powerful when we focus intention, but it still works, nonetheless. Begin repeating these words in order: "I'm sorry, please forgive me, thank you, I love you." You can also put *I love you* first like this, "I love you, I'm sorry, please forgive me, thank you." It is recommended to say it 108 times, like you would do with a mantra. If there is a particular person you are wanting to forgive, you can say their name in the prayer: "John, I'm sorry, please forgive me, thank you, I love you." If you want to practice self-forgiveness, say your name in the prayer: "Allison, I'm sorry, please forgive me, thank you, I love you." This technique works best if you practice it daily. I experienced noticeable shifts in my relationships and my life using this prayer.

Buddhist Prayer of Forgiveness – I love this prayer. It basically sums up everything I have written about in this chapter in four powerful sentences. I have a printed copy of this prayer on my wall in my office as a beautiful reminder that we all do the best we can with the level of awareness that we are at in the moment. We are all imperfectly perfect. <u>How to do it:</u> Get into a comfortable position in a quiet space. Take some nice, deep relaxing breaths. When you are ready, read the prayer aloud:

If I have harmed anyone in any way either knowingly or unknowingly through my own confusions, I ask their forgiveness.

If anyone has harmed me in any way either knowingly or unknowingly through their own confusions, I forgive them.

And if there is a situation I am not yet ready to forgive,
I forgive myself for that.
For all the ways that I harm myself, negate, doubt, belittle myself,
judge or be unkind to myself through my own confusions,
I forgive myself.

Lineage Prayers – (These prayers were written by Howard Wills).

Lineage prayers are a powerful way to clear ancestral karma and DNA and release family patterns and struggles. The study of epigenetics shows that traumas and unresolved emotions were imprinted onto our parents' and ancestors' nervous systems and are passed down from generation to generation. Generational karma that we receive from our lineage is in our DNA. Think about your family patterns – alcoholism, depression, abuse, illnesses, money issues, or victim consciousness – all stem from generational karma, our ancestral DNA. By incorporating lineage prayers into our daily practice, we can heal and clear these karmic issues. <u>How to do it:</u> Get into a comfortable position in a quiet space. Take some nice, deep relaxing breaths. When you are ready, read the prayers aloud.

Prayer to cleanse relationships with all women:
For all of the women who have ever hurt me, I forgive you, all of you. Mother(s), mother(s)-in-law, daughter(s), daughter(s)-in-law, sister(s), sister(s)-in-law, aunt(s), grandmothers, friends, ex-lover(s)/ex-wife(s), partner(s), wife. I ask that you all please forgive me. Divine Light, please help us all to forgive each other and to forgive ourselves. Let us all forgive and release ourselves for our hurts, wrongs, and mistakes to ourselves and to others. Please, Divine Light. Thanks, Divine Light. Amen.

Prayer to cleanse relationships with all men:
For all of the men who have ever hurt me, I forgive you, all of you. Father(s), father(s)-in-law, son(s), son(s)-in-law, brother(s),

brother(s)-in-law, uncle(s), grandfathers, friends, ex-lover(s)/ex-husband(s), partner(s), husband. I ask that you all please forgive me. Divine Light, please help us all to forgive each other and to forgive ourselves. Let us all forgive and release ourselves for our hurts, wrongs, and mistakes to ourselves and to others. Please, Divine Light. Thanks, Divine Light. Amen.

General Lineage Forgiveness Prayer:
Divine, for me and my entire lineage throughout all time, past, present, and future: please help us all forgive all people, help all people forgive us, and help us all forgive ourselves. Please Divine. Thank you, Divine. Amen.

Forgiveness Affirmations – Positive affirmations are a great way to ease into forgiveness, especially if you are feeling stuck or have resistance to it. Affirmations rewire the neural pathways in the brain that are creating blocks or fear, and form new pathways for positive thoughts and behaviors. By repeating the affirmations on a daily basis, you will begin to move past the resistance and gradually become more open to the forgiveness process. <u>How to do it:</u> Affirmations can be done pretty much from anywhere – on your couch, in a chair, from your bed, on a walk, and so on. Wherever you feel most comfortable. It is best to state them out loud, in the present tense, and repeat them at least once or twice a day. Once in the morning and once in the evening is best. If there are one or two affirmations that stand out for you, feel free to say them to yourself throughout the day to reinforce those new neural pathways you are building.

The past is gone and I live only in the present now.

I live in the moment of now and create my life the way I want it.

I follow the principle of live and let live.

As I forgive myself, it becomes easier to forgive others.

As I follow the path of forgiveness, I can draw my new life plan and move forward as I wish.

Each day is a new opportunity.

Today is the first day of my new life free from the past.

I forgive everyone from my life in the past and love myself into the future.

I move beyond forgiveness to understanding and I have compassion and kindness for all.

I am forgiving, loving, gentle, and kind.

I am safe in the knowledge that life loves me.

I easily forgive others and I am easily forgiven.

I forgive myself and release my past.

I forgive and communicate love, easily and effortlessly now.

I now liberate my past from my mind, body, and spirit. I am free!

I forgive my family and embrace them with love and compassion.

I am deeply loved and forgiven.

I release the past and look forward to the future.

My forgiving nature is contagious.

I set my past free and forgive myself for my participation.

I am willing to forgive.

I release myself from my anger and let the past go.

The past is forgiven and I am thankful.

I let go of my hurt and anger toward others.

I allow divine love to permeate my thoughts.

I live in the now each moment of each day.

Today, I choose to forgive myself.

My memory of this situation is healed.

Forgiveness Meditation – Listening to meditations on forgiveness is helpful when you are trying to heal and move on from past hurts. Meditating allows your conscious mind to step aside so that you can access your subconscious and heal old patterns, beliefs, and habits. It can be a very healing process on all levels – body, mind, spirit, and emotions. <u>How to do it:</u> Get into a comfortable position in a quiet space and begin to take some nice deep, relaxing breaths. Imagine that you are in a room with two chairs and then when you are ready, bring in the person you would like to forgive. While you are both sitting in the chairs, begin to tell this person whatever is on your mind right now. Let them know how hurt or angry you are. This is a safe, loving space and you have all the time you need to express your feelings. Once you are finished, you can then imagine this person saying to you whatever it is that you need to hear in order for you to heal and move on. When they are finished, imagine any cords or connections to this person being cut and removed with love, thank them for coming, and then imagine them leaving or you can leave them there if you prefer. You can repeat this process as often as you need to and bring in different people if needed to continue your healing and forgiveness process.

Forgiveness Worksheets – Worksheets on forgiveness can provide a higher perspective on our feelings and beliefs when it comes to being hurt or angry, feeling like a victim, or wanting to blame others. They can be quite helpful in releasing stuck emotions, shifting perspective, and taking your power back. <u>How to do it:</u> Find a private, quiet, comfortable spot where you can take time to reflect on the person or situation that you want to forgive. Fill out the worksheets and then read them out loud if you are able to. This really helps with shifting the vibration of the situation and clearing out any stuck emotions. You can fill out as many worksheets as you need for as many people or situations that you need to heal from. I found that sometimes I needed to use the worksheet multiple times for one person or situation if it was something that I was having difficulty letting go of. There is no right or wrong way to do this, just trust your inner guidance with this.

Chapter 14

Step 7 – Self-Love and Self-Care

"Love is the most healing force in the world; nothing goes deeper than Love. It heals not only the Body, not only the Mind, but also the Soul."

– Osho

For years I would tell my clients that they needed to practice self-care, that they could not have authentic, loving relationships with others if they did not love themselves. "Put yourself first," I would say, "and quit running yourself ragged doing everything for everyone else. You will never find someone who places you first in their life if you are always putting yourself last." I would give them the airplane oxygen mask analogy that we all know and love – *put your own mask on first before assisting others* – then send them out the door with some affirmations, a link to a guided meditation I recorded on this topic, and homework to incorporate self-care into their daily lives. After my client left the office, I

189

would make a mental note to listen to my own advice because it was an area of my life I struggled with. I almost always felt run-down and exhausted from trying to help everyone, take care of my family, achieve my goals, and not taking time for myself.

It truly is great advice. But for many of us, especially women, we have been taught and conditioned to believe that it is not OK to put ourselves first or take time out for self-care. We often watched our mothers, grandmothers, and others who we looked up to in our lives, take care of everyone and everything. Generation after generation this was the role of women in the family, staying home cooking, cleaning, and managing the household. During the feminist movement in the 1960s until the late 1970s, women entered the workplace and began to pursue careers of their own. While this paved the way for future generations of girls to have the freedom to achieve their goals and dreams, it also left a gap in the caretaker role in the household. If mothers were working, who was home managing everything? Women faced a no-win situation with having to choose between career and family. Obviously, that was not an option many were willing to accept, so they took on both, usually with little to no support from their husbands or other family members. Women gained their rights, freedom, and independence to pursue careers and demand equal pay, but somewhere along the way, they lost the belief of being worthy and deserving of time to take care of themselves.

Fulfilling multiple obligations perfectly is an impossible situation that often leads to burnout, meltdown, or breakdown. Superwoman Syndrome is a term that was coined in 1984 by Marjorie Hansen Shaevitz in her book of the same name. Superwoman Syndrome occurs when a woman neglects herself as she strives to achieve perfection in every role she is fulfilling. Juggling career and home, managing a never-ending to-do list, being a loving mother and spouse, fulfilling social obligations, and living up to the expectation to excel in all of these areas comes at a cost – mentally, emotionally, physically, and spiritually.

It is just not feasible to function at this level for any sustained period of time. Studies show that girls as young as 13 can be affected by Superwoman Syndrome. The pressure and stress of trying to be everything to everyone can become dangerous and unhealthy. Maintaining high levels of stress can lead to ulcers, migraines, high blood pressure, and heart problems, as well as unhealthy coping mechanisms such as over or undereating, increased alcohol use, or shopping and overspending. Women may also rely on prescription drugs such as stimulants and anxiety medication or increase caffeine intake throughout the day to keep going.

Emotional and cognitive symptoms of stress:
- Irritability
- Inability to concentrate
- Memory problems
- Mood swings
- Constant negative thinking
- Emotional outbursts
- Indecisiveness
- Lack of sense of humor

Physical symptoms of stress:
- Muscle tension
- Stomach/abdominal pain
- Muscle spasms or nervous tics
- Unexplained rashes or skin irritations
- Sweating when not physically active
- Butterflies in stomach
- Unable to sleep or excessive sleep
- Shortness of breath

Many people misunderstand the concepts of self-love and self-care. They believe that it is about being selfish or having a "me, me, me" mentality or that self-care is only about getting a massage and manicure. Believe me, it is much, much more than that! If you have grown up or lived with a narcissist, it can be hard to embrace the idea of putting yourself first after years of placating, people-pleasing, and denying your own needs. Some women may view the neglect of their needs as a badge of honor that they wear with pride. This only leads to resentments and frustration toward others. Self-care is an absolute necessity for recovery from trauma and living a fulfilling and healthy life. While self-love and self-care are different, they are intertwined and necessary to one another. Let's take a look at what each of these terms mean and then we will delve into how to incorporate self-love and self-care practices into our daily lives.

Self-love was a completely abstract concept to me that felt like it should have been obvious, but whenever I tried to think of it in terms of myself, I felt like a kindergartner trying to understand astrophysics. Self-loathing I was intimately familiar with, but self-love was elusive and vague to me. I got that it was critically important, I just didn't know how to pull it into my reality. The Merriam-Webster Dictionary defines self-love as a) "an appreciation of one's own worth or virtue" and b) "a proper regard for and attention to one's own happiness or well-being." Self-love is loving yourself unapologetically, all of you – flaws, mistakes, warts, and all. Period. There are no conditions or circumstances that must be met to be worthy of this love. It just is. No excuses, no negotiating or compromising with others about it. It is 100 percent authentically loving YOU, in this moment right now, no matter what. I finally get this one now and I live it daily. It is truly an amazing experience feeling comfortable in my skin and having compassion and love for myself regardless of what is going on in my life.

Self-care is a major component of self-love and is the action of loving and caring for yourself. It has become a trendy topic and has been described by some as simply having a spa day with your girlfriends or eating chocolate cake if you want it. Sure, those could be considered self-care, but it goes way beyond that. The truth is that self-care is at the forefront of our minds because we are exhausted, run-down, and desperate to find ways to cope in the hectic world we live in. In order to fully step into loving yourself, you need to consistently incorporate self-care into your daily routine. Not just for the physical body but for the mind, spirit, and emotions as well. Self-care is also about setting healthy boundaries for yourself and others. Nobody really talks about this, but sometimes it is about doing things you don't like or don't want to do because that is what is in your best interest.

Actual self-care is more than occasionally treating yourself to a bubble bath or pedicure. True self-care is about no longer using our crazy busy lives as an excuse to procrastinate or avoid making changes for the better. It is choosing not to make an impulse purchase because you made a commitment to yourself to save for retirement or pay off debt. It is forgoing watching more episodes of the Netflix show you love and putting yourself to bed at a decent hour so you can get 8 hours of sleep. It is saying no to doing things that you don't want to do and saving your energy for the things that truly matter to you.

When you start gradually taking the steps toward real self-care, you begin sending messages to your mind, body, and spirit that you are present. You are no longer abandoning yourself and your needs when you get triggered, and instead you double down on your self-care efforts. You completely remove yourself from the toxic cycle of numbing, distracting, or escaping by making a solid commitment to yourself and your life. You become a loving, but firm, parent to yourself and consistently make positive, healthy choices for your long-term well-being. When this happens, you will notice a powerful shift in your view of yourself, your life, and how the world perceives you as well. Your inner world is aligned with your outer world, and you feel peace in your heart. Self-love is no longer a vague, abstract concept. It is your reality and you live it wholeheartedly on a daily basis.

Now that you have a deeper understanding of self-love and self-care and how they are both absolutely necessary to experience a healthy, fulfilled life, it is time to put them into practice. Self-care feeds into self-love, and self-love helps with prioritizing your needs for long-term well-being. The following ideas and practices will help with incorporating self-care into your daily routine. Keep in mind that it does not need to be done perfectly. The key here is doing it consistently until self-care becomes a habit and daily priority for you; when it becomes so ingrained in your life that when you skip or miss a day, something feels "off." Some of these practices will be a review from previous chapters since all the steps in this healing process can be considered components for self-care. This last step is the culmination of everything you have been practicing so far and brings it all together so you can create a lovely daily routine for yourself.

I have also included some ideas for what I call "extreme self-care." Extreme self-care is for those times when you know you have pushed yourself right up to your breaking point or perhaps even past it and need emergency TLC. You can even plan ahead for extreme self-care downtime when you've got an event coming up that you know will tap you out – physically, mentally, and emotionally – and know you will need to unplug and have some alone time so you can recharge your batteries. For some people this could be after traveling, family gatherings, holidays, or completing big work projects.

Finally, I have separated the ideas and practices for self-care into categories of body, mind, spirit, and emotions. Some of these practices are repeated from previous chapters, but I wanted to have them all in one place for you to easily reference. Feel free to skip over these if you have already reviewed or incorporated them into your daily routine.

While we should always try to consistently care for all areas and strive for balance in each of those parts of ourselves, sometimes we need to focus our attention on a certain aspect that is off balance. For example, maybe you are doing a really great job caring for your physical body – choosing healthy foods, getting enough sleep, and exercising – but you are feeling disconnected, lost, and without purpose. It would be helpful to put some extra focus into the self-care of spirit practices. Or perhaps you are feeling really tuned in and your intuition and mind are sharp and flowing, but you have been neglecting your physical body in favor of more intellectual or spiritual interests. If that is the case, focus more on self-care for the physical body to bring things into balance.

Self-Care for the Body:

Epsom Salts Bath – Taking baths with Epsom salts has tremendous benefits, and I do this at least three to five times a week to soothe, heal, and relax my body. I lived with pain and inflammation for over 15 years, so this was a must-have in my self-care practice. Bathing with Epsom salts, which contain magnesium, provides benefits such as soothing aches and pains, reducing inflammation, relieving stress, relieving constipation, and aiding with more restful sleep. How to do it: Pour one to two cups of Epsom salts into your bathwater. You can also put them into the running water if you want them to dissolve more quickly. For extra healing benefits, you can add essential oils to the water such as lavender, chamomile, frankincense, ylang ylang, and citrus. (Avoid essential oils if you are pregnant, nursing, or for infants under one year of age).

Breathwork – People who have experienced trauma or are under chronic high levels of stress tend to have very short, shallow breathing. I don't know why it's called breath*work* because it is one of the quickest and easiest ways to calm your nerves, energize, and center yourself. Pranayama is a yogic term for control over the energy in the breath. It provides quick and efficient ways to tap into the nervous system. Research has shown how breathwork relieves stress and anxiety and helps with trauma recovery.

Calming Breath: Use this before bed, at work, or anytime you need to calm your nervous system. How to do it: Place one hand on your heart and one hand on your belly. Inhale through the nose counting to five, then exhale through the nose counting to five. Make sure that the breath is going through the diaphragm into the belly, and not the chest. You'll feel the rise and fall of your belly as you breathe in and out. Do for a minimum of 3 minutes.

Alternate Nostril Breathing: This type of breathing calms, balances, and unites the right and left sides of the brain. Great for releasing fatigue and tension. How to do it: Start in a comfortable meditative pose, hold the right thumb over the right nostril and inhale deeply through the left nostril. At the peak of inhalation, close off the left nostril with the ring finger, then exhale through the right nostril. Continue the pattern, inhaling through the right nostril, closing it off with the right thumb, and exhaling through the left nostril.

15-Second Breath: This breathing exercise soothes fear and helps with cognition. <u>How to do it:</u> Begin by inhaling slowly for 5 seconds, filling the lower abdomen, stomach area, lungs, and then finally, the chest. Hold the breath in for 5 seconds and then slowly exhale for 5 seconds. Increase the number of seconds counting 10-10-10 when you feel comfortable. Do for a minimum of 3 minutes.

Dragon Breath: This is an energizing breathing technique and great when you wake up in the morning. <u>How to do it:</u> Begin in a comfortable seat and sit up tall. Breathe through your nose during this breathing exercise. Relax the muscles of the stomach. Take a deep inhalation through the nose and then exhale through the nose. Begin to breathe rapidly in and out through the nose and pump the navel point in and out with each breath. Maintain an equal emphasis on the exhalation and inhalation. The breath should be shallow, so it can be quick. Caution: this is an energizing exercise – if you are already experiencing high stress, rapid heart rate, or anxiety, choose one of the calming breathing techniques above.

Mindful or Meditative Yoga – This type of yoga is a great way to calm the mind and feel safe and present in the body. The main goal of this type of yoga is that it engages the body in a mindful way. Trauma-sensitive yoga, mindful yoga therapy, qigong, and meditative flow are some types of movement that can provide trauma healing through mindful movement. How to do it: Start with something slow and simple. I recommend finding a studio or videos that are focused on mindful and meditative yoga practices. I started my yoga practice with a 7-minute meditative flow. This was perfect for me in the beginning because I was totally resistant to yoga in the first place, and my excuse was always that I never had enough time. Well, 7 minutes is easy to make time for, and I loved how I felt afterward, especially in such a short amount of time!

Joyful Exercise – Exercise can be healing and nourishing for the body, when it is done in a mindful, loving, and joyful way. Many people approach exercise with dread or view it as a chore, something that has to get done, but has very little joy in it. I used to pound my body into the ground running or working out every day, mostly out of habit or fear that if I didn't do it, I would gain weight. Interestingly, studies show that we receive much greater benefits from exercise when we voluntarily do it than we feel obligated to do so. Forced or obligatory exercise increases stress and cortisol response in the body compared to those who exercise out of desire or choice. I have completely shifted how I approach my daily exercise and workouts. Now I choose to only do the things that bring me joy or that I love doing. The activities I enjoy the most are running, yoga, tennis, and softball. I also like strength training if I have a partner to do it with me. I am no longer obsessive about my workouts or force myself to do them. This has created a huge shift for me in how I care for my body and my mindset going into the activity. How to do it: Make a list of activities that you enjoy or love doing. Move your body in ways that are joyful and fun for you, several times a week for at least 30 minutes. The options are limitless, but here are a few suggestions to get you started: take a class such as dancing or karate or yoga, take up gardening, get outside and go for a hike or a walk in nature, roller skate, jump rope, join a tennis league, take a swimming lesson, learn tai chi, have a friend join you, listen to uplifting or inspiring audio recordings while you joyfully move your body, take a hula or belly dancing class, go for a bike ride with your kids or play with them at the park.

If it has been a while since you've gotten your body up and moving, start slow and gently. This is not a race or competition. The point is to have fun and enjoy yourself so that you'll stick with it and get healthy – in body, mind, and spirit. Start with 5 minutes and gradually add one or two minutes each time until you are able to consistently spend 30 minutes in joyful body movement, at least three times a week. If you tend to overdo it, or if you are an over-exerciser, it may be difficult to cut back on your current routine. Ask yourself if you are really enjoying it, or if it is just habit. Explore your emotions by asking yourself what would happen if you cut back or changed up your routine to incorporate some joyful body movement. If fear or anxiety arises with these thoughts or questions, don't judge yourself but just notice it and see if you can uncover what is underneath the fear or anxiety. What is really going on here? Once you have an idea of what is driving you to over-exercise or why you fear changing your routine, you can work on healing it and begin incorporating joyful body movement into your life.

Massage Therapy – Sure, a little bit of pampering is nice but including massage in your self-care routine can also have positive benefits for your physical body. I have had a monthly membership for massages for the past five years and it has helped me reduce the chronic pain, inflammation, and stress in my body. Other benefits of massage therapy are improved circulation, elimination of toxins, improved flexibility, improved sleep, reduced fatigue, and improved immunity. How to do it: Research massage places near you that offer monthly memberships. They usually offer a discounted rate for your first massage so you can try it out and if you like it, you can sign up. Most places do not require contracts and are typically month to month. One thing that is important to keep in mind though, with this membership, is that you need to make an appointment and *actually* go to it. It is easy to make excuses about being too busy to take time for it. Make the appointment, put it on your calendar, and show up for your hour of self-care. If you know someone who is a massage therapist and you are not able to pay for a monthly membership, you could offer to trade services with this person. I did this quite often when I was first starting out in my holistic wellness business and money was tight. I gave them a Reiki or hypnotherapy session in exchange for a massage.

Body Oiling – Abhyanga is the Ayurvedic art of massage with healing oils and can be done by a practitioner or by yourself at home. The benefits of body oiling include improved circulation, strength, vision, stamina, softer skin, strengthened body tissues, improved tone and skin appearance, and better sleep. How to do it: It is good to apply the oil to your body after using a dry brush. The dry brush preps the skin to receive the oil. Select the type of oil you want to use. Traditional ayurvedic practice recommends certain oils depending on your ayurvedic body constitution – kapha, pitta, or vata. To keep it simple though, coconut oil is typically used in the late spring, summer, and early fall, or for those people who have excess heat in their system, as it has cooling properties. Sesame oil is used in the late fall, winter, and early spring or for people who tend to have more cold in their systems. You can do this practice daily, although you will still receive great benefits from body oiling if done just two to three times a week.

Steps to Perform Self-Abhyanga

1. Brush your skin with a dry brush to remove dead skin, dirt, and debris from its surface as well as prepare the skin's pores for receiving the oil.

2. Warm your oil – you can do this while dry brushing if warming your oil in a pot, or rub the oil between your palms if you are short on time.

3. Gently but firmly, massage your body all over: Begin with the neck, working your way down to your feet. Use long strokes for limbs and short strokes for joints. Don't forget fingers and toes and pay extra attention to the soles of your feet, as they contain all the nerve endings and important marma points, or conjunctions of prana, life force energy.

4. Let the oil sit for 5–10 minutes. Don't skip this step, as abhyanga's deeper benefits depend on the body's absorption of the oil and herbs. It takes a few minutes for the oil to penetrate to the deepest layers of the skin, and several minutes more for it to penetrate the tissues of the internal body. This is an excellent time to prepare some tea or practice some deep breathing.

5. Rinse excess oil with a cool shower on warm days, or a warm shower (but not hot) on cold days. Don't skip this step either, as excess oil will clog the pores.

Get Enough Sleep – I know this one seems obvious and it gets preached to us constantly from health, beauty, medical, and mindfulness experts. It seems like a no-brainer. Go to bed at a reasonable hour, sleep deeply, and then wake up refreshed and ready for the new day. Unfortunately, this is not the case for approximately 50 to 70 million Americans who suffer from some type of sleep disorder. In 2008, the CDC stated that insufficient sleep is a public health epidemic. Over 70 percent of American adults report insufficient sleep for at least one night a month, and 11 percent report insufficient sleep every night. These are startling, but not surprising, numbers given our fast-paced, high-stress lifestyles that leave little time for rest or relaxation. Our health and well-being depend on good sleep.

Benefits of Getting a Minimum of 8 Hours of Sleep:

1. Reduces stress and cortisol levels

2. Improves memory

3. Lowers blood pressure

4. Improves immune system

5. Helps with weight loss and maintenance

6. Reduces risk of type 2 diabetes

7. Reduces pain and inflammation

8. Regulates hormones

9. Increases energy

How to do it: Individuals who have experienced trauma frequently struggle with sleep issues, which have a detrimental effect on health and well-being. It is especially important for your self-care routine to take the proper steps to get enough sleep each night. Once you have established a nightly routine and your body begins to adjust to a consistent bedtime, so many things will fall into place for you. Getting enough sleep is the foundation from which to build. Here are some tips for getting a better night's sleep:

1. Stick to a sleep schedule of the same bedtime and wake up time, even on the weekends.

2. Practice a relaxing bedtime ritual.

3. If you have trouble sleeping, avoid naps, especially in the afternoon.

4. Exercise daily.

5. Design your sleep environment to establish the conditions you need for sleep.

6. Sleep on a comfortable mattress and pillows.

7. Use bright light to help manage your circadian rhythms.

8. Avoid alcohol, cigarettes, and heavy meals in the evening.

9. Spend the last hour before bed doing a calming activity.

10. Keep work materials, computers, or televisions out of the bedroom.

11. Use your bed only for sleep and intimacy to strengthen the association between bed and sleep.

12. Record your sleep in a sleep diary to help you better evaluate common patterns or issues you may see with your sleep or sleeping habits.

Nourish and Hydrate Your Body – There are thousands of books written on this topic, so I'm not going to go very in-depth on this one. We all have a fairly good idea of what foods best nourish our bodies and which ones do not. Because of my eating disorder history and my own resistance to other people forcing their diet beliefs on me, I tend to be very reluctant to give my clients advice regarding what to eat and what not to eat. I have a popular 6-week course on holistic weight loss called the "Holistic Weigh" and I still don't give food recommendations. Every body is different and we are all at different places in the trauma healing process.

During my trauma healing journey, I knew exactly what I should eat for my body to run at its optimal state, yet I still often ate foods that were comforting in order to soothe my anxiety and chronic pain. It wasn't until I made self-care a priority and continued releasing trauma from my body that I was able to eventually make healthy food choices and nourish my body consistently. If you struggle in this area like I did, my recommendation is to find what works for you and try to stop judging yourself so harshly for not being able to stick to a healthy diet. Do your best to drink more water and make healthy food choices most of the time, and then trust the process. Eventually, it all will click into place as you consistently incorporate other self-care practices into your daily routine.

Body Acceptance and Gratitude – This is a great practice for your self-care toolbox. It can be challenging to go from self-loathing, constantly at war with your body, or being frustrated that it isn't as healthy or functioning as well as you would like to unconditional love and acceptance of it. Many of my clients struggle with this issue and rather than have them work on loving their body right out of the gate, I have found that starting with acceptance, appreciation, and gratitude works wonders in removing resistance and getting more positive results.

I once heard Louise Hay, one of my favorite authors, say that our bodies are like racehorses or slaves, and we can try to whip them into submission and beat them over and over to do our bidding and they will do their best to comply because they want to please us and make us happy. And it may work for a little while, but eventually they get worn down, and tired of being whipped, disrespected, berated, and belittled. Then they either give up or rebel. But when we offer them encouragement and love and praise, and honor and respect them, they are happy and have energy and perform above our expectations. Incorporating body acceptance, appreciation, and gratitude allows us to begin the process of healing the relationship with our bodies and move toward a more loving and peaceful coexistence.

How to do it: Get in a comfortable position and take in some nice, deep, relaxing breaths. Begin by scanning your body and sending love to any areas of your body that may be feeling discomfort. Then starting with the top of your head, think of ways that you are grateful for each part of your body, until you reach your toes. Include your muscles, organs, nerves, and so on. "I'm grateful for my arms because they allow me to hug my loved ones." You can also thank your body for everything it does for you; feel free to name examples such as beating your heart, breathing, or turning food into fuel. When you are finished, imagine a pink light surrounding your entire body, flowing through you and all around you.

Affirmations for Body Appreciation

I nurture and pamper my body with love.

I am perfect, whole, and complete just the way I am.

I love and respect my body.

My body is a temple. It is easy to treat it with love and respect.

I have everything inside of me that I need to take care of my body.

A goal weight is an arbitrary number, how I feel is what's important.

I am worthy of love and so is my body.

The only opinion of my body that matters is my own and I'm doing the best I can.

I no longer compare myself to others. It is OK to be me just the way I am.

It's OK for me to like my body. It's OK for me to love my body.

I love and appreciate my body for all that it does to support me.

It's OK for me to trust the wisdom of my body.

I release the past and treat my body with love and appreciation now in the present moment.

I can choose the way I want to live my life and treat my body.

I easily maintain balance by listening to my body for signs of going too fast.

I enjoy feeling good about myself. It's OK for me to feel good about my body.

Being skinny or fat is not my identity. I am who I am on the inside, a loving, wonderful person.

I choose health and healing over diets and punishing my body.

It's OK to let others love my body.

My very existence makes the world a better place.

My well-being is the most important thing to me.

I am responsible for taking care of my body.

I can be conscious in my choices for caring for my body.

My body is healthy, fit, and strong.

My body can be healthy at any size.

My body is wise and guides me to knowing what it needs.

It's OK to let my mind and my body relax.

I am a human being, not a human doing. It's OK to just be sometimes.

My body is a vessel for my awesomeness.

I am grateful for my healthy and strong body.

My needs are just as important as anyone else's.

I can take of myself and my needs without feeling guilty.

I easily make peace with my body and appreciate it for all that it does for me.

I feed my body life affirming foods so that I can be healthy and vital.

Taking care of myself and my body feels good.

I get plenty of sleep and wake up each day feeling refreshed and full of energy.

The numbers on the scale are irrelevant to who I am as a human being.

My body deserves to be treated with love and respect.

It is safe for me to be present in my body.

My body loves and supports me and I am safe, now and always.

The Body Acceptance Pledge

I, _____, vow to follow this body acceptance pledge to the best of my ability and I will give myself grace, patience, and understanding as I learn a new way of living with myself and my body.

I promise to start loving my body, however I am feeling, however I look, whoever I'm with, and wherever I am.

I promise to replace negative thoughts about myself and my body with positive ones because I know that not everything I think is true.

I promise to stop participating in group body bashing of myself and others. Instead of tearing others or myself apart, I will make every effort to say positive things about myself and others.

I promise to stop comparing myself to others because I know

that everyone's body is different, including my own.

I promise to stop hurting my body with overeating, over-exercising, or by not feeding it or nurturing it in loving ways.

I promise to honor and respect my body and care for it in positive, healthy ways.

I promise to stand up for myself or others when I hear negative or harmful things, including those things in my own mind.

I promise to let go of any ideas I have about the perfect or ideal body, or how my body "should" look.

I promise to accept compliments about myself without trying to brush them off, downplay them, or feel unworthy of them.

I promise to practice gratitude and appreciation for my body each day.

Self-Care for the Mind:

Guided Meditation – These are great to begin with because you can just sit or lie down while listening to someone else guiding you through the meditation, and it gives your mind something to focus on. Listening to someone else's voice in meditation, just like what would occur in a hypnotherapy session, provides a distraction for the conscious mind so that healing can take place under the surface in the subconscious mind.

Guided meditations come in many different formats and cover a variety of topics from relaxation to healing to spiritual journeys. You may find as you try out different guided meditations that you like some people's voices, or music, or style better than others. I have a couple of dozen of my favorites and rotate what I listen to depending on my mood or needs at the time.

Positive Affirmations – Using positive affirmations can be a powerful technique for improving your life on many levels. The mind's ability to program itself is extremely powerful! Even if at first it seems like what you are affirming isn't true, stick with it and before you know it you'll start feeling more relaxed as you go through your day, more comfortable in your body and your surroundings, and develop courage in being able to move forward toward healing. As Wayne Dyer said, "You'll see it when you believe it," which means that as you start changing your negative inner self-talk to the positive, your outside world begins to change for the better.

You may notice how people react in a more positive way toward you, opportunities present themselves unexpectedly, and positive situations manifest consistently on a daily basis. You will begin to trust the process and know that everything is working out for your best and highest good and know that you are surrounded by love and protection – now and always! This is the power of using positive affirmations! Napoleon Hill once stated: "Whatever the mind of man can conceive and believe, it can achieve." How to do it: You can listen to these affirmations anytime – in the morning when you first wake up, before falling asleep at night, in the car, while exercising or anytime that's convenient for you. Here are some tips that will help make these affirmations even more powerful:

First – Listen to them daily: at least once per day, but in the morning and in the evening is best.

Second – Say the affirmations out loud: the power of the spoken word is much more powerful than thoughts in your head or words on paper.

Finally – Commit to doing the affirmations for a minimum of 21 days: if you wish to keep doing them that's wonderful … but it takes around 21 days to form a new habit and shift the old ways of thinking.

Gratitude – Most people understand that being grateful contributes to living a happier life, but gratitude can be a powerful tool for the mind because it can actually rewire the neural pathways in the brain and shift negative thoughts, beliefs, and patterns! It's literally impossible to complain and be grateful at the same time. Gratitude has been shown to reduce depression and anxiety, increase relationship satisfaction, and increase resilience in times of stress or difficult situations. When you practice gratitude, you raise your vibration and begin attracting *more* things to be grateful for. It's also a quick and easy exercise that you can do in just a few minutes each day. How to do it: There are a number of ways to incorporate gratitude into your daily routine. You can try them all or stick with whichever one you like, but be sure to consistently do them for at least 30 days.

Positive Thought Momentum – This exercise is a great way to begin shifting habitual negativity into positive thoughts. If you can hold positive thoughts for 68 seconds, it builds a positive thought momentum. Building up the momentum of each positive thought in sequence and holding the thought in your mind allows you to strengthen the neural pathways in your brain that are focused on the positive. How to do it: Begin by writing down four positive statements of things that you want to manifest in your life. The positive thoughts can be general or specific. Ideally, the statements are on the same goal or intention, and they build on one another in sequence. Repeat the first statement over again for 17 seconds, then move to the second statement and repeat it for 17 seconds and continue doing the same thing for the third and fourth statements. Once you finish all four statements, sit in the energy of the positive thought momentum for 3 minutes. For example, you might say, "I take excellent care of my body" and keep repeating it for 17 seconds, then "I am comfortable in my body" and repeat that for 17 seconds, then say "I love and appreciate my body for all that it does for me" and repeat for 17 seconds, and finally repeat "I am at peace with my body" for 17 seconds. Then hold on to the positive feeling of the vibration of those statements for 3 minutes.

Mantras – Saying mantras is a great way to help with a busy mind, looping or obsessive/anxious thoughts, or when negativity hits. Looking at the root meaning of the word, *man* means "to think or thinker" and *tra* means "tool or instrument," so it basically translates into "a tool for the thinker." Mantras calm and center the mind and help relieve symptoms of anxiety, stress, and depression. A mantra is usually a Sanskrit word, phrase, or sound that is repeated in a mindful or meditative way, although I've seen them translated and said in English as well. Some people like to create their own mantras and say those too. I prefer the traditional Sanskrit mantras, as I believe there is a sacredness and higher vibration in the words and phrases when uttered in their original form that was created thousands of years ago.

Mantras are often repeated 108 times, which is a sacred number in Hinduism and yogic traditions. There are a couple of explanations for the significance of 108. First, the numbers 1, 0, and 8 represent one thing, nothing, and everything (infinity), and when the numbers are combined into 108, it represents the reality of the universe as being simultaneously one, emptiness, and infinite. Also, Vedic mathematicians calculated the distance between the Sun and the Moon to the Earth as 108 times their respective diameters.

How to do it: In a comfortable, seated position with your back tall and straight, begin the process of repeating a mantra of your choice. There are mantras for protection, abundance, peace, removing obstacles, and health. You can repeat your mantras to recordings and follow along, which is a great way to learn the pronunciation and flow of the words, or you can practice them silently in your head. Saying them out loud sends the vibration throughout your physical body, which adds healing benefits. Repeating them quietly in your head requires extra focus attention, which adds additional mindfulness benefits. You can also use mantras during activities such as walking, hiking or driving, and they are still effective as long as they are practiced with love, awareness, and attention. I like to use mala beads when saying mantras. Malas, or prayer beads, are a string of 108 beads and are used for counting as you repeat each mantra. Many malas have dividers placed at the quarter and halfway marks along the string of beads that give you the option of doing a shorter number of mantras if time doesn't allow for the full 108 repetitions.

Take a Break from Social Media – We all occasionally need some downtime from scrolling through our social media accounts. Too often we compare our lives to others on these platforms and feel like we don't measure up to the standards we see from our virtual perspective. While social media can be a great way to connect and find support and community, it can also generate quite a lot of negativity regarding social and political issues among "friends." Studies show that too much screen time can negatively affect our mental health, increasing depression and anxiety. Taking some time away from this provides less screen time overall and a reprieve from the drama and time spent scrolling through posts and advertisements. We then have the opportunity to focus on the present moment and spend quality time with the important people in our lives.

Tips for Taking a Break from Social Media:

1. Put your phone down and out of reach.

2. Track your social media time and set limits for yourself.

3. Turn off notifications.

4. Create phone-free zones in your home.

5. Schedule social media time.

6. Delete social media apps from your phone.

7. Catch up with friends or family by calling or meeting in person.

8. Find hobbies that you enjoy and keep your mind off your phone.

9. Get out in nature and leave your phone behind.

De-Clutter and Create Sacred Space – Taking time to get organized and getting rid of items that you no longer need helps with productivity and a positive mindset. When there is an order to your surroundings, it creates a sense of peace and calm, reducing anxiety. It is also easier to find items and makes life run a little more smoothly. When we clear out our closets and donate clothes or household items that we do not need anymore, not only are we helping others who might need those things, but we create space to breathe and think, and for new and positive things to come our way. Holding on to clutter blocks our energy, releasing it opens the flow of energy.

Create a sacred space in your home where you can go to relax and enjoy peaceful time for yourself. Place sacred objects, artwork, statues, incense, candles, pillows, and blankets, or anything else that you find soothing in this space. I have two rooms in my home that I dedicate to sacred space. One is my office where I meditate and pray, create my writings and recordings, have sessions with clients, and do yoga and breathwork, and the other is my bathroom where I take soothing baths with incense, candles, and peaceful music. Everyone in my family knows that this is my sacred space and time, and they are respectful of that and rarely disturb me unless it is an emergency. When I get this time for myself, I am much more centered and present for everyone else in my life.

Re-scripting – This exercise expands on the observer mind technique by taking the thought pattern and underlying belief and changing the story. This is especially helpful for those who have experienced trauma, since they often get stuck in powerlessness because they were unable to or were prevented from taking action at the time of the trauma. Re-scripting works because the brain doesn't know the difference between what is imagined and what is real, so we can rewrite the story with actions that are empowering and provide closure.

How to do it: In a comfortable, seated position take in some calming and relaxing breaths. Gently close your eyes and focus your intention on the thought pattern and its underlying belief that you would like to rewrite. As you tune in to the negative or limiting belief, ask yourself where this belief may have come from. Allow yourself to remain open and curious as you receive the answer. Continue to gather more information such as whether this was your belief or was it taught to you, did it come down through your family, or was it created through an event or experience. As you receive the answers, continue to stay in observer mind without judgment. If any memories come up while you're exploring the origin of the belief, allow yourself to remain unattached as you observe the memory. Now imagine changing the outcome of that memory … perhaps you need to bring in another person to help, or maybe there are things you have to say that you weren't able to at the time. Take a few moments to play out the memory the way you want it to … you are in charge. Good. Now think about what you needed and didn't get at that time. Was it a hug, some comfort or reassurance … an acknowledgment or apology … a friend or loved one to talk to so you could feel heard and supported. Take some time now to give yourself whatever you needed. Good. Once that feels complete, replace the old belief with a new positive statement. Repeat the positive statement several times and allow it to flow over your body like a warm blanket. When you feel ready, open your eyes and bring your awareness back to the room.

Creative Visualization – The practice of using visualization for desired outcomes is a popular technique used by athletes, business coaches, and law of attraction gurus. Incorporating a daily routine of visualizing your desires as if you are already living them can greatly accelerate the achievement of your goals and dreams. There are several benefits to using visualization: it increases creativity, programs the brain to seek out resources needed to achieve the goal, activates the law of attraction to bring those resources to you, and increases motivation to take action to accomplish your goal. How to do it: Get into a comfortable position either lying down or in a chair. Taking some nice, deep, relaxing breaths. Begin to imagine what your life would look like if your goals and dreams had already been achieved. How you would feel, who the people are with you, and the smells or sounds – incorporate this vision as vividly as you possibly can. You can also imagine that you are watching your life play out on a giant movie screen. Once you are finished, bring your awareness back to the room. You can follow this activity up with positive affirmations to help keep you focused on achieving your goals.

Self-Care for the Spirit:

Spend Time in Nature – Taking the time to be in nature is one of the best gifts you can give yourself. Studies show that spending just 30 minutes in nature has amazing benefits such as improved memory, decreased depression and anxiety, improved concentration, reduced stress, strengthened immune system, and improved overall mood. How to do it: Pick a place that calls to you – the beach, the mountains, your local park, a nature trail, or even your backyard. Dedicate the time to really experience the benefits of your surroundings including smells, sounds, and the pleasant feeling of connecting with nature. Plan this time in your schedule each week. Take a quick 30 minutes outside in your neighborhood or make a day trip out of it and venture to a local destination you have been wanting to visit. Better yet, schedule a longer trip to one of your favorite locations to really boost your time in nature and soak up that healing and relaxation.

Get Involved with Community – I have found when working with clients that one of the frequent areas of discontent they experience is feeling disconnected. Practicing self-care for the spirit is a surefire way to reestablish or boost that connection with the divine. In our hectic lives that rely heavily on technology for communication, it is easy to feel isolated and lonely. Joining a community with like-minded people offers that connection and support that is often missing in our lives. Belonging to a spiritual community offers many benefits such as connection to others, support when we are struggling, inspiration, motivation to improve our lives, and a place where we feel safe and secure to be ourselves. How to do it: There are a plethora of options to choose from when it comes to spiritual communities, so it is important to be discerning and find one that feels right for you. Meetup is a great resource for finding groups and you can search by the type of group you are looking for. Churches, yoga classes, meditation centers, and spirituality courses are all excellent places to find communities with like-minded people. Once you have found some options that resonate with you, schedule a tour, go to a group meeting, or sign up for a class!

Start Creating – Taking inspired action and creating something is one of the quickest ways to practice self-care for spirit. When we create, whether it is writing, drawing, painting, cooking, sewing, gardening, or dancing, we are channeling a divine connection through us. Feeling inspiration and cocreating with the divine is a joyous and beautiful experience and quickly restores balance in our spiritual connection. How to do it: Tune in to your heart and take some time to contemplate creative outlets and activities that you enjoy doing or feel inspired to learn more about. Watch instructional videos, take a dance or painting class, or trust the divine wisdom flowing through you and begin a project you have been inspired to work on. Don't worry about doing it right or perfectly. If it is coming through the divine, it is already perfect.

Trust Your Gut – Intuition is a natural part of our being, but we often second guess ourselves and doubt that "inner voice" when it is telling us something. We have been taught to think and make decisions based on logic, not by what our gut says. As we begin to trust that inner knowing and have success following it on a consistent basis, we build a stronger relationship with ourselves and our divine connection. There are many benefits to trusting your intuition such as gaining confidence in yourself and your decisions, focus and clarity in difficult situations, increased creativity, being more in tune with your physical body, recognizing the messages and nudges when they come to us, and experiencing less fear and worry knowing we are being divinely guided.

How to do it: Listening to and trusting your intuition is a skill that needs to be developed, so it requires regular practice. As you become aware of a gut feeling or intuitive guidance about something, act on it right away, and continue to do this each time so it feels more comfortable and your confidence continues to grow. Incorporate mindfulness and meditation into your daily practice as they help strengthen intuition. Guidance and messages can come through dreams, so pay attention to your dreams and keep a notepad by your bed to write down any notes or observations from your dreams upon awakening.

Pray and Meditate – It is said that prayer is talking to the divine, and meditation is listening for the response. When we incorporate both practices into our daily self-care routine, we open the lines of communication with the divine going both ways. Prayer and meditation lift our consciousness and align us with our highest selves and the divine. With this connection, we are able to release the pain of the past, trust that we are fully supported by the universe, and move forward with purpose in our lives. How to do it: Find a quiet, comfortable space where you can have uninterrupted time for yourself. Take some deep, relaxing breaths and visualize yourself surrounded by a crystalline, divine, white column of light. Begin by saying or reading your prayers. I like to use forgiveness prayers, lineage prayers, gratitude, or the ho'oponopono prayer. Once you are finished with your prayers, move into the meditation. You can sit in silence, count your breaths, repeat a mantra, or listen to guided meditations, whatever works best for you.

Chakra Balancing – There are seven main chakras that are located along different points on the body, and they are connected to various organs and glands within the body. Each of the chakras carries a specific meaning, is associated with a color, and influences different areas of our life and health. Stress, lifestyle, negative thoughts, habits or patterns can create a disturbance or block in the energy flow of chakras. When a chakra is disrupted or blocked, the life energy also gets blocked, and it creates issues in our lives on all levels – physical, emotional, mental, and spiritual. People who have experienced trauma often have disruptions or blocks in their chakras due to the negative effect that trauma has on their minds and bodies. Because of this, it is important to take time to clear and balance these energy centers in order to restore the natural flow of life energy.

How to do it: Gently close your eyes and take in some deep, relaxing breaths. Bring your awareness to your root chakra. Notice if you're aware of any blocks or imbalances there, and if there are, visualize a ball of red light in the area of your root chakra slowly rotating clockwise. See it clear and bright and perfectly balanced. Next, focus your attention on your sacral chakra. Again, notice if there are any blocks or imbalances there and visualize a ball of orange light in this area, clear and bright and balanced. Continue working your way through each chakra clearing and balancing them as you go. When you are finished, visualize a column of white light surrounding you, infinitely up and infinitely down, flowing through you and all around you. Practice this daily at first until you feel like there are minimal blocks or disturbances, then just do this as needed when you are feeling imbalanced.

Violet Flame Visualization – The great thing about the violet flame is that it is easy, quick, and efficient to use and you can do it from anywhere. It is made up of love (pink), wisdom (gold), and power (blue), and when these are combined, they create the violet flame. Violet is the highest vibrating color of transmutation, fire is the fastest form of transformation, and together they become an amazing way to transmute, transform, and transcend lower vibrating energies, thoughts, patterns, and beliefs. It helps remove resistance, clear negativity, and elevate your vibration so that you can come into alignment with your intentions and desires. If you are feeling skeptical, or you have never heard of or worked with the violet flame, give it a try for a few weeks and see what type of shifts take place in your life. How to do it: Gently close your eyes and take in a few deep, relaxing breaths. Visualize a column of white light surrounding you, flowing infinitely up and infinitely down. Then picture the violet flame surrounding you, flowing through you and all around you. You can say aloud, "I call upon the violet flame to surround me now to clear my energy and raise my vibration." When you're ready, give yourself permission to let go of and release any lower vibrating energies, thoughts, patterns and beliefs, and send them into the violet flame to be transmuted and transformed. Continue releasing what is no longer serving you – any negativity, negative emotions, obstacles or blocks, lack or limitation, or anything else that has been keeping you stuck. Send it into the violet flame. If you have a specific intention for the violet flame, state it aloud. This could be something like "Please clear any fear and anxiety now," and then release it to the violet flame. You can end the process saying "Thank you. And so it is. Amen" or whatever feels right to you. Repeat as often as you need to!

Read or Listen to Uplifting Material – There are so many wonderful inspirational books and audiobooks, videos, podcasts, and music to choose for this self-care practice. I am always reading several books, listening to audiobooks, positive affirmations or music in my car while I'm driving or cleaning the house, and watching motivational videos on YouTube. It is consistently a part of my daily routine and essential for me in maintaining a positive mindset. How to do it: Make a list of motivational and inspirational books that you want to read or listen to. You can check them out at the library, read as an e-book, or listen to as an audiobook. Create a collection of uplifting audio recordings such as mantras, spiritual music, podcasts, or positive affirmations. Set aside time to incorporate these into your self-care practice each day.

Self-Care for the Emotions:

Journal – Using a journal to write down your feelings is a great way to use self-care for the emotions. Journaling helps you track patterns or triggers so you can be prepared or resolve them more quickly. It has been shown to reduce stress, anxiety, and depression. A journal is also a great place for increasing self-awareness, clarifying thoughts and feelings, and improving problem-solving skills. Writing in a journal on a regular basis can improve the immune system and keep your memory sharp.

How to do it: Find a comfortable, quiet, and private space where you can take some time to record your thoughts, feelings, or experiences. You can use any kind of notebook or paper, nothing fancy is required for this exercise. I was resistant to journaling for years because I thought if I opened up to my feelings that I might not be able to switch them off. So, to motivate myself to begin the daily writing process, I bought some nice leather-bound journals and colorful pens. If you do not know what to start writing about, try beginning with writing about the events of your day. If you are struggling with self-esteem issues or depression, you can write down positive affirmations about yourself and your life or things you are grateful for. Here are some tips for beginning (or restarting) a daily journaling practice:

1. If you are concerned about getting too deep into your feelings, set a timer for a few minutes to start with and then see how things are going. If you are doing well, set the timer again for a few more minutes. If you are struggling and feel like you might get sucked under with too much emotion, shift your focus to positive affirmations or a gratitude list. Revisit the topic another time.

2. Write about challenging or triggering events in the third person.

3. Before beginning the journaling practice, imagine that you are surrounded by divine white light or a ball of pink divine love. Know that you are fully loved, supported, and protected as you go through this writing process.

4. If you are feeling stuck with what to write about, start writing your thoughts in the moment. That might even begin with *"I don't know what to write about but I know Allison said that journaling is supposed to be a great practice for self-care and so I'm giving it a shot even though I'm not quite sure what I think or feel about it right now."* It is OK to ramble on. Keep going without judgment or worrying about what is being written down. Pretty soon the words will begin flowing in a more confident and natural style for you.

5. Be honest. There is no need to worry about what people think or trying to look your best and appearing perfect on paper. This is just for you and your personal growth and development.

6. Write about your goals and dreams. Give yourself permission to think big and really go for it.

7. Journal daily. A consistent practice of writing down your thoughts and feelings has tremendously positive benefits and can create huge shifts in your self-awareness, intuition, and overall emotional well-being.

Feel and Heal Process – Begin by getting into a comfortable position, either seated or lying down. Take in some nice, deep relaxing breaths and follow the steps below.

1. *Invoke Mindful Awareness or Sacred Presence* – If you've been practicing mindfulness, take a moment to get centered and grounded, and shift your awareness into the present moment. You can also call in the divine or sacred presence (whatever that is for you) and surround yourself in a cocoon of divine white light and protection. Feel the white light flowing through you and all around you, feeling safe and secure ad protected.

2. *Identify the Feeling/Emotion* – As you sit for a few moments, become aware of what the feeling or emotion is that you are experiencing. You can say it out loud or in your head. If you are connecting to a feeling in your body such as exhaustion or hunger or pain, what would this translate into if it was an emotion or feeling?

3. *Sense the Feeling/Emotion in Your Body* – Once you've identified what the feeling or emotion is, notice where you are experiencing it your body. Is it a knot in your belly, a tightness in your chest, a lump in your throat? Give yourself a few moments to become aware of where the feeling is in your body and just notice it without judgment.

4. *Sit with the Feeling/Emotion* – Take some time to sit with the feeling or emotion. Allow yourself to really feel it in your body. There may be some discomfort at first but give yourself time to allow it to come to the surface so it can be released and let go.

5. *Accept it* – Acknowledge the feeling or emotion you're experiencing. You might like to investigate a little further and ask what you can learn from it or how you can grow from the situation or experience.

6. *Reframe it* – Sometimes a memory comes up when we are processing emotions, particularly when we tune in to the sensations in the body. Because our bodies hold trauma and memories, they may come to the surface while we go through the process. Think about how you could rewrite or reframe the outcome. Was there something that needed to be said that you weren't allowed or able to say at the time? Was there something

you needed in the situation like a supportive friend or someone there to help you? Did you need to take some type of action like remove yourself from the situation or stand up for yourself? Take a few minutes to reframe the memory with what you needed at that time. Really feel the shift take place from feeling powerless or like a victim to feeling strong and fully supported and protected by the divine.

7. *Release it* – Now, with gratitude for the lesson and healing, take a few deep, calming breaths and allow yourself to release and let it go. Allow it to come to the surface, flowing out of your body and away from you, sending it into the violet flame to be transmuted and transformed. Or you can visualize it floating down a stream or river until it completely disappears. Take as much time as you need until the process feels complete.

8. *Repeat if Needed* – Sometimes when we go through this process, there are underlying emotions beneath the feeling or emotions we just released. If this happens, go back to step 1 and begin the process again so that you can release the underlying emotion as well. I've found that anger may be an initial emotion that covers up hurt or sadness, or that worry/anxiety may cover up fear or shame. As you continue to work through the Feel and

Heal process, you'll notice it gets easier and more comfortable with consistent practice.

Self-Esteem Affirmations – If you struggle with feelings of not being good enough, self-loathing, or dislike certain aspects of yourself, self-esteem affirmations are an effective practice to rewire the neural pathways in your brain to create new, positive thoughts and beliefs about yourself and your life.

How to do it: You can use affirmations any time – on first waking up in the morning, in the shower, in the car, while on a walk, or during your daily self-care routine. It is best to do them at least twice a day for a minimum of 30 days, so they become a habitual way of thinking for you. Say them out loud if possible. This gives them vibration, makes them more powerful, and shifts negative thoughts and beliefs more quickly.

Today I am capable of handling anything that happens.

I am attracting great things into my life.

I am confident and strong.

I am supported by the universe.

I feel good about who I am.

I am a unique and priceless person.

My life is wonderful.

I love myself.

I am a happy, positive person.

I am worthy.

I'm capable of creating and maintaining a great life.

I deserve to have a great life.

I am beautiful inside and out.

I'm capable of changing my life for the better.

I'm worthy of being treated well.

I'm worthy of a great life.

I am a divine being of light.

My family loves and supports me.

My friends are always there for me.

I am creative and interesting.

I am perfect just the way I am.

I can change my life story whenever I want.

I have the right to change my life to suit my personal needs.

The movies in my mind are wonderful because I choose to make them so.

Today I am taking steps toward a happier life.

I have a wonderful circle of friends.

I am a caring person with lots of friends who care about me.

I accept myself for who I am.

I can trust and rely on myself.

I am unconditionally loved by the universe.

I am fully competent and capable.

I honor and respect myself.

My worth as a human being is unconditional.

I am respected and well-liked by all the people that I know.

I accept and rejoice at my individuality.

I respect myself, I respect others, and others respect me.

I trust myself completely.

People like to be around me.

I create my own reality.

I can say no to other people.

I have healthy personal boundaries.

Everyone is special, including me.

It is OK for me to be good to myself.

I can put myself first without feeling guilty.

If I need something, it is OK to give it to myself.

I have the right to be happy and healthy.

I spend time in meaningful ways.

My relationship with my family is better than ever.

I forgive myself and look forward to the future.

Others value me just for being who I am.

All of my dreams are coming true.

Today I treat myself like a queen.

What matters most is what I think about myself.

I live my life according to my own beliefs and values.

Other people honor and appreciate who I truly am inside.

I am my own best friend.

I listen to myself and I trust myself.

I accept myself.

Heart Meditation – This is a great exercise for learning how to drop down into your heart. You will become aware of what it feels like to be in the energy of the heart, and the wonders that you can tap into while you are there. This is where divine power, love, and wisdom reside and where you can access deep levels of your intuition and subconscious. Being present in this sacred space is what it truly means to live from the heart. <u>How to do it:</u> Sitting with your eyes closed, taking in some nice, deep and relaxing breaths, gently place both hands over your heart. Begin to feel a warm, comfortable, and loving light in your hands and as this light grows, feel it spreading into your heart. Allow it to flow into your heart space and fill your chest area, bringing a sense of peace, calm, and healing to your entire body. Ask your heart what it needs to hear right now to feel love and acceptance. Listen for the answer and then say the words to your heart, either out loud or in your mind. Feel your heart accepting the kindness and love, then sending it throughout your entire body. Imagine a pink light flowing through you and all around you. This pure divine love filling every cell of your body. As this pink light is flowing through you, notice how lovely it is to feel so loved and connected in this moment. Sit with this for a few moments as you allow this feeling to settle in. When you are ready, give thanks to your heart and the divine, and open your eyes.

Self-Compassion – Many of us were taught to be hard on ourselves in order to get motivated to do better or be better. We criticize, put down, belittle, or shame ourselves for not living up to the high standards and expectations we have set for ourselves and our lives. Practicing self-compassion helps us silence the inner critic and develop a kind and accepting attitude toward ourselves. Kristin Neff, a leading research on self-compassion, identified three elements to self-compassion:

1. **Self-kindness** – helps let go of self-judgment and the inner critic and replaces it with a kinder, gentler voice that supports and encourages you.

2. **Mindfulness** –reduces negative thought patterns and behaviors and increases self-awareness that supports growth and change.

3. **Common humanity** – gets us out of victim or narcissistic thinking and reminds us that we are all human and experience challenges and setbacks as a part of our learning and growth process.

Radical Acceptance – This is one of my favorite practices for emotional self-care. It completely changed the way I react to and deal with challenges, disappointments, and setbacks. Ruminating about situations or events that we cannot change or have no control over creates unnecessary suffering. Beating ourselves or others up over something that happened in the past perpetuates the cycle of pain. Radical acceptance helps with letting go and moving on and brings freedom and peace to your life. When we completely and totally accept something exactly the way it is right now, we are no longer giving it our energy or trying to control it. This process frees us from powerlessness and a victim mentality. We become empowered by radically accepting ourselves and our lives with a kind and compassionate heart.

How to do it: Find a comfortable and quiet space and begin by closing your eyes and taking in some deep, relaxing breaths. Imagine yourself surrounded by a bubble of divine white light, flowing through you and all around you. Feel safe, loved, and protected as you are being held in this divine light. Become aware of any areas of your life where you might be resisting or fighting reality. Some may be at the front of your mind and others may be a little less obvious. Consider situations or events you may be bitter or resentful about. Perhaps this is sometimes thinking your life should not be this way, that if a situation changed or something went differently then you could be happy. Maybe you are frustrated or unhappy with life, and people often disappoint you. Think about ways you may try to control situations or behaviors of others or expect other people to change to make you happy. Good. Now that you have an awareness of areas you may be resisting, shift your focus to acceptance. Take some calm, relaxing breaths, breathing peace and calm into your heart. Say to yourself or out loud, "I am willing to accept." Notice any tension or tightness that you might be holding in your body and continue breathing peace and calm into your heart, sending it throughout your entire body. Continue saying to yourself or out loud, "I am willing to accept myself, my life, and these situations exactly as they are," until you feel your body relax and let go. When you are ready, bring your awareness back to the room and open your eyes. Repeat this practice as often as you need to.

Say No – Being a people pleaser often means having a difficult time saying no to others when they ask for help. Helping people and being kind, caring, and compassionate is a wonderful trait to have, but everyone has a limit on their time, energy, and how much they can do in a day. People pleasers often overextend themselves and have a hard time setting boundaries for themselves and with others. They often have a fear of rejection and do not want to cause other people to feel hurt or angry. Saying "no" can cause feelings of guilt or regret. On the other hand, not saying "no" enough can cause stress, reduce immune function, and lead to exhaustion and feelings of resentment. It is critically important for our well-being and emotional self-care to set boundaries for ourselves and others.

The Benefits of Saying "No"

1. **Reduces Stress** – Taking care of others and neglecting your own needs causes anxiety, stress, tension, and exhaustion.

2. **Frees up time** – More time for self-care, family, and activities that you really enjoy.

3. **More energy** – Increased energy and better performance in your work and home life.

4. **Eliminates toxic people in your life** – People who were only wanting your help or time without reciprocation on their part disappear when they are no longer receiving what they want from you.

5. **Better sleep** – Reduced stress, tension, and overtaxing from helping others too much allows for more restful and deeper sleep.

6. **Builds confidence** – Setting proper boundaries for yourself and others sends a message that you are strong and taking care of yourself. The more often you do it, the easier it gets, and the better you feel. Honoring yourself and your needs gains respect from others and often leads to their encouragement and support.

How to do it: First, remember that saying no is not rude or selfish. Your self-worth is not tied to how much you do for others. It might help to visualize yourself saying no, especially if it is difficult or uncomfortable for you. See yourself successfully saying no with confidence and kindness, being firm and direct with your response. You can also practice with a friend. It is not necessary to provide reasons or excuses why you are saying no. We often do this because we feel guilty or do not want to hurt other people's feelings. Be honest and sincere. People appreciate and respect a "no" response over someone who agrees out of obligation and ends up resentful about it. The more often you take care of yourself by saying no, the easier it becomes. Once this becomes a comfortable self-care practice for you, you will find that you say yes to things you really want to do, and life becomes much more joyful as a result.

Chapter 15

Step 8 – Keep Moving Forward

"If you can't fly then run, if you can't run then walk, if you can't walk then crawl,

but whatever you do you have to keep moving forward." – Martin Luther King, Jr.

The quote for this chapter is one of my favorites. It perfectly describes my attitude about the healing process. I would say to my therapist, "Well, it isn't pretty or graceful, but I'm making forward progress." Sometimes I used the football analogy and would say I was gaining positive yardage. Even if I was just inching forward at the pace of a snail, I considered it a win. It was not always like this for me though. I never thought of myself as a steady-as-she-goes kind of person. The tortoise in the race with the hare? Definitely not.

Generally speaking, I had two levels of functioning: 1) 100 percent full speed ahead, all systems go, focused, determined to accomplish whatever I set my mind to, and 2) OFF. There was no grey or middle ground for me. I was in or I was out. Black and white, all-or-nothing thinking was my jam. You needed a top-performing, number one in the division, highest number of sales, achiever on your team? I was your gal. Well, that is until I wasn't. Eventually, I would burn out, lose interest, give up, and collapse into a ball of anxiety, exhaustion, and unworthiness. I approached everything I did like this. Dieting and exercise, household projects, to-do lists, business endeavors, creative projects, and relationships. I gave it everything I had until I didn't have anything left to give.

Healing from trauma is a messy process. There is no straight line from point A to point B. It is often a zigzagging, two steps forward and three steps back, spiraling journey that keeps you disoriented and unsure if you are making any headway whatsoever. It is easy to feel shame and hopelessness around the lack of progress in your healing journey. When we are feeling stuck, we compare ourselves to others who are doing OK or who picked themselves up after a traumatic experience and moved on with their lives. We think we have healed and moved on from something. Then we get triggered and have a knee-jerk reaction to an old pattern or behavior that causes us to question whether we have really made any progress in this area.

There is no one size fits all solution to healing trauma. Each person's experience is unique and varies whether they experienced a single trauma or years of ongoing trauma and neglect. Some people have better resilience skills and can move through setbacks more quickly. Sometimes there are bigger lessons to learn that require more attention and rounds through the healing process. Some traumas are multilayered and need finesse and delicate handling while working through them. We have to let go of the self-judgment and comparison as we go through our own individual healing journeys. There is often enough judgment and stigma with the trauma itself, so we do not want to add any more obstacles for us to overcome during our healing process.

What I found to be one of the most important steps over the course of my thirty-plus year journey of healing was simply to keep going. To keep moving forward, no matter what. Crawl if necessary. Looking back, I realize I was unnecessarily hard on myself for not progressing or doing the healing process like I thought I was supposed to. I made things too complicated. I searched for that one book, training, or guru that was going to finally be the answer. I experienced healing therapies that triggered me and sent me scurrying back inside myself for months. I tried avoiding the issues so that I could avoid the pain as well. But the numbing and distracting only last so long before they eventually become another problem to deal with. When I finally accepted that the only way through is through, I made the commitment to myself to face it head-on with my eyes open. There was still a part of me that was skeptical. A part that thought perhaps it was not possible to heal and it really was just a matter of managing symptoms as best as possible.

Throughout all of the different things I tried and did during my healing journey, the one thing that remained a common factor was that I kept trying. I kept going. Even if I felt stuck or hopeless, I still went to the appointments, read the books, and did the exercises. Not daily at first, but eventually it got there. I would get triggered and hunker down in fear for a while, then dust myself off and keep going. After a few years of that, I decided not to use getting triggered as an excuse to stop taking care of myself. I wrote out a healing manifesto and read it frequently. In it I stated that I would make my self-care and healing a priority in my life, *especially* if I was feeling triggered. This is when it really clicked for me. I thought I was taking care of myself by hiding out, but I was really abandoning myself by throwing my daily practices out the window when I got triggered.

These past few years I have really noticed a shift in how I approach pretty much everything in my life now. I take things at a much slower pace, no longer leaving a trail blazing behind me as I push myself to exhaustion and burnout. I have more than two levels of functioning now, with various settings that I adjust according to how I am feeling and what messages my body is sending me. I practice self-care daily and extreme self-care when needed, and I set healthy boundaries for myself and others so that I can keep this commitment. I used to take pride in being an Energizer Bunny, always going and doing. Now I am thrilled to be the slow and steady tortoise, living in the moment, and taking time to focus on the things that are most important to me.

If there is one thing I cannot emphasize enough as you begin to incorporate these steps into your healing journey, is that it does not matter if you do them well or if you do them perfectly. Just find some of them that work for you and do them. Keep doing them. Try different combinations of practices. Have some longer routines, and shorter ones for the days you don't have as much time available. Make a commitment to yourself to do them. Keep freaking going. Because in a month, in six months, and in a few years from now you will look back and see what a massive difference this has made to your life.

"A river cuts through rock, not because of its power, but because of its persistence." – James N. Watkins

Here are some examples of different daily practice routines that you can play around with and see what works best for you. I found that some weeks I enjoyed incorporating a lot of yoga into my morning practices, and then other weeks I would do more meditation and mantras and do very little or no yoga. I believe that we intuitively know what we need, so listen to that inner voice that is guiding you. Create your own routine and trust the process. There is no right or wrong, nothing needs to be done perfectly, and there is no order or amount of time that has to be followed. This is your time dedicated to your self-care and healing, so do what feels good to you and see what happens.

Example Daily Practice Routines:

<u>30-Minute Daily Practice:</u>
Calming Breathwork
7-Minute Meditative Flow Yoga
Ganesh Mantra – Om Gum Ganapatayei Namaha (Removing of Obstacles)
Ho'oponopono Prayer
Violet Flame Meditation

Energizing Breathwork
Ganesh Mantra
Journey Into the Heart Meditation
Self-Esteem Affirmations

Calming Breathwork
7-Minute Meditative Flow Yoga
Feel and Heal Process
Violet Flame Meditation

40-Minute Daily Practice:
20-Minute Meditative Flow Yoga
Forgiveness Prayers
Destination Vibration
Self-Love Affirmations

Calming Breathwork
Healing Mantra – Om Shree Dhanvantre Namaha
Positive Thought Momentum
Ho'oponopono Prayer
Deep Relaxation and Healing Meditation

Energizing Breathwork
7-Minute Meditative Flow Yoga
Journey Into the Heart meditation
Ganesh Mantra
Gratitude Journaling

60-Minute Daily Practice:
20-Minute Meditative Flow Yoga
Healing Mantra
Positive Thought Momentum
Feel and Heal Process
Lineage Prayers
Violet Flame Meditation

Calming Breathwork
7-Minute Meditative Flow Yoga
Ganesh Mantra
Destination Vibration
Forgiveness Meditation
Gratitude Journaling

Calming Breathwork
Positive Thought Momentum
Journey Into the Heart Meditation
Radical Acceptance
Forgiveness Prayers

Morning and Evening Routines

If you do not have time or it feels too overwhelming to do everything in one sitting, I have found that breaking the practices up into a couple of time blocks works great. Many of my clients enjoy starting and ending their days with a few of the practices. Here are a couple of examples of morning and evening routines. Again, feel free to customize it with the practices that work best for you depending on which areas need the most attention right now.

Morning
20-Minute Meditative Flow Yoga
Ganesh Mantra
Violet Flame Meditation
Self-Esteem Affirmations

Evening
Epsom Salts Bath With Essential Oil
Forgiveness Prayers
Journey Into the Heart Meditation

Morning
Calming Breathwork
7-Minute Meditative Flow Yoga
Heart Mantra
Destination Vibration Meditation

Evening
Body Oiling With Warm Shower
Gratitude
Positive Thought Momentum
Self-Love Affirmations

Morning
Energizing Breathwork
7-Minute Meditative Flow Yoga
Violet Flame Meditation
Body Oiling With Warm Shower

Evening
Ganesh Mantra
Forgiveness Prayers
Chakra Clearing and Balancing Meditation

Take some time to plan out your daily practices. There is a planner included in the downloadable materials that you can use to plan your daily practices, make notes on your experiences, and what routines work best for you.

Type of Practice	Morning/Evening	Observations

Additional Resources

Here are some additional resources that complement the 8 steps for trauma healing. I am not affiliated with these companies, websites, or programs in any way. I am just including them here as an additional resource for you to explore if you wish to.

Trauma-Sensitive Yoga

Calo Programs – Trauma Center Trauma Sensitive Yoga
TCTSY is an empirically validated, adjunctive clinical treatment for complex trauma or chronic treatment-resistant PTSD. In 2017, TCTSY became the first dedicated yoga program in the world to be listed as an evidence-based program/practice for the treatment of psychological trauma.

For more information:

https://caloprograms.com/trauma-center-trauma-sensitive-yoga-tctsy.html

https://www.traumasensitiveyoga.com/

Heart Math Institute

Studies show that practicing HeartMath tools can lead to better reaction times, improved sleeping habits, revitalized energy, a stronger immune system, and so much more. They have a free program you can do to give it a try.

For more information:

https://www.heartmath.org/training/

Law of Attraction

I love the teachings of Abraham-Hicks and I started reading their books back in the early 2000s. If you want to learn more about manifesting and raising your vibration to attract positive things into your life, this is a great place to start.

For more information:

https://www.abraham-hicks.com/

DBT – Dialectical Behavior Therapy

This is a type of cognitive behavioral therapy developed by Marsha Linehan in the late 1980s. Its main goals are to teach people how to live in the moment, cope with stress in a healthy way, regulate emotions, and improve relationships with others. It was originally intended for people with borderline personality disorder (BPD), but has been adapted for other conditions where the person struggles with emotional regulation or exhibits self-destructive behavior, such as disordered eating, substance misuse, and post-traumatic stress disorder (PTSD).

There are a ton of books on this topic. If you want to read about Marsha Linehan and how she developed DBT, here is a link to her memoir: https://www.amazon.com/Building-Life-Worth-Living-Memoir/dp/0812994612
To find a certified DBT practitioner:
https://dbt-lbc.org/index.php?page=101163

Radical Forgiveness

This book by Colin Tipping was written in 1997. It has helped people heal personal wounds, gain greater connection with their spirit, and to help heal the planet. I read this book in 2010 and used the worksheets for years for myself and my clients. My forgiveness and self-forgiveness worksheets are based on Tipping's work.

There are a ton of free tools available on the Radical Forgiveness website: http://www.radicalforgiveness.com/free-tools/

Mirror Work

I used to have a ton of resistance around doing mirror work, which is looking at yourself in a mirror while saying positive affirmations. I have found that it is a very effective way to learn to love yourself and see the world and your life in a loving way. Saying affirmations when you are in front of a mirror is very powerful. The more you do it, the better the relationship with yourself will become. Louise Hay published a book on mirror work and there is a 21-day online video course on Loving Yourself. Louise passed away in 2017 but her work still helps thousands of people every day.

For more information:

https://www.louisehay.com/what-is-mirror-work/

Ayurveda Body Types (Doshas)

I touched on this very briefly in the chapter on self-love and self-care. Knowing more about your Ayurvedic body type can help with the trauma healing process. There are three main types (vata, pitta, and kapha) and then a few combination types as well. Learning the beneficial times for sleep, practices for body care, best ways to calm or energize, and when you are most productive can make your daily practices more effective.

For more information:

https://kripalu.org/content/whats-your-dosha

References

Ackerman, C. (2020, April 28). *83 Benefits of Journaling for Anxiety, Depression, and Stress.* Positive Psychology. https://positivepsychology.com/benefits-of-journaling/

American Psychiatric Association. (2013). *Diagnostic and statistical manual of mental disorders (5th ed.).* Washington, D. C.: Author.

Bonanno, G. A. (2004, January). *Loss, trauma, and human resilience: have we underestimated the human capacity to thrive after extremely aversive events?* PubMed. https://pubmed.ncbi.nlm.nih.gov/14736317/

Bonanno, G. A. (2007, October). *What predicts psychological resilience after disaster? The role of demographics, resources, and life stress.* PubMed. https://pubmed.ncbi.nlm.nih.gov/17907849/

Brach, T. (2004). *Radical Acceptance: Embracing Your Life With the Heart of a Buddha* (Reprint ed.). Bantam.

Braden, G. (2015). *Resilience from the Heart: The Power to Thrive in Life's Extremes* (Revised, Updated ed.). Hay House Inc.

Bradshaw, J. (2005). *Healing the Shame that Binds You (Recovery Classics)* (Revised ed.). Health Communications Inc.

Briggs, R. (1999). *Transforming Anxiety, Transcending Shame* (1st ed.). HCI.

Brown, B. (2010). *The Gifts of Imperfection: Let Go of Who You Think You're Supposed to Be and Embrace Who You Are* (1st ed.). Hazelden Publishing.

Brown, B. (2012, March). *Listening to shame.* TED Talks. https://www.ted.com/talks/brene_brown_listening_to_shame?language=en

Brown, R. P., & Gerbarg, P. L. (2012). *The Healing Power of the Breath: Simple Techniques to Reduce Stress and Anxiety, Enhance Concentration, and Balance Your Emotions* (1st ed.). Shambhala.

Byrne, R. (2006). *The Secret* (10th Anniversary ed.). Atria Books/ Beyond Words.

Canfield, J. (2019, December 2). *Visualization Techniques to Manifest Desired Outcomes.* Jack Canfield. https://www.jackcanfield.com/blog/visualize-and-affirm-your-desired-outcomes-a-step-by-step-guide/

Cloitre, M., Courtois, C. A., Ford, J. D., Green, B. L., Alexander, P., Briere, J., Herman, J. L., Lanius, R., Stolbach, B. C., Spinazzola, J., Van der Kolk, B. A., Van der Hart, O. (2012). The ISTSS expert consensus treatment guidelines for complex PTSD in adults.

Courtois, C. A., & Ford, J. D. (2009). *Treating complex traumatic stress disorders: An evidence-based guide.* New York: The Guilford Press.

Curran, T., & Hill, A. P. (2019). Perfectionism is increasing over time: A meta-analysis of birth cohort differences from 1989 to 2016. *Psychological Bulletin, 145*(4), 410–429. https://doi.org/10.1037/bul0000138

Dyer, W. W. (2005). *The Power of Intention* (1st ed.). Hay House Inc.

Eastman, L. E. (2007). *Overcoming the Super Woman Syndrome* (1st ed.). Professional Woman Publishing.

Ferrari, M., Yap, K., Scott, N., Einstein, D. A., & Ciarrochi, J. (2018). Self-compassion moderates the perfectionism and depression link in both adolescence and adulthood. *PLOS ONE, 13*(2), e0192022. https://doi.org/10.1371/journal.pone.0192022

Fortuna, J. L. (2010, June). *Sweet preference, sugar addiction and the familial history of alcohol dependence: shared neural pathways and genes.* PubMed. https://pubmed.ncbi.nlm.nih.gov/20648910/

Gibson, L. C. (2015). *Adult Children of Emotionally Immature Parents: How to Heal from Distant, Rejecting, or Self-Involved Parents* (1st ed.). New Harbinger Publications.

Guiley, B. R. E. (2020, January 27). *The Importance of Prayer and Meditation*. Unity. https://www.unity.org/resources/articles/importance-prayer-and-meditation

Harvard Health Publishing. (2010, July). *Spending time outdoors is good for you, from the Letter*. Harvard Health. https://www.health.harvard.edu/press_releases/spending-time-outdoors-is-good-for-you

Hawkins, M. D. P. D., & David R. Hawkins, M. D. P. D. (2013). *Power vs. Force*. Penguin Random House.

Hay, L. (1995). *Heal Your Body*. Penguin Random House.

HeartMath Institute. (n.d.). *Chapter 01: Heart-Brain Communication*. https://www.heartmath.org/research/science-of-the-heart/heart-brain-communication/

Herman, J. L. (1992). *Trauma and recovery: The aftermath of violence from domestic abuse to political terror*. New York: Basic Books.

Hicks, E., & Hicks, J. (2006). *The Law of Attraction: The Basics of the Teachings of Abraham* (1st ed.). Hay House Inc.

Jacobs, J. M. (2008, April). *Going outdoors daily predicts long-term functional and health benefits among ambulatory older people*. PubMed. https://pubmed.ncbi.nlm.nih.gov/18332184/

Kabat-Zinn, J. (2013). *Full Catastrophe Living How to Cope with Stress, Pain and Illness Using Mindfulness Meditation [Paperback] Jon Kabat-Zinn* (Revised edition). Little, Brown Book Group.

Kolk, V. B. (2015). *The Body Keeps the Score: Brain, Mind, and Body in the Healing of Trauma* (Reprint ed.). Penguin Books.

Levine, P. A., & Mate, G. (2010). *In an Unspoken Voice: How the Body Releases Trauma and Restores Goodness* (1st ed.). North Atlantic Books.

Neff, K. (2015). *Self-Compassion: The Proven Power of Being Kind to Yourself* (Reprint ed.). William Morrow Paperbacks.

PhD, P. S. G. (2010). *Present Perfect: A Mindfulness Approach to Letting Go of Perfectionism and the Need for Control* (1st ed.). New Harbinger Publications.

Porges, S. W. (2017). *The Pocket Guide to the Polyvagal Theory: The Transformative Power of Feeling Safe (Norton Series on Interpersonal Neurobiology)* (1st ed.). W. W. Norton & Company.

Scaer, R. (2014). *The Body Bears the Burden: Trauma, Dissociation, and Disease* (3rd ed.). Routledge.

Schucman, S., & Helen Schucman, S. (2007). *A Course in Miracles*. Foundation for Inner Peace.

Self-love. (n.d.). The Merriam-Webster.Com Dictionary. https://www.merriam-webster.com/dictionary/self-love

Shaevitz, M. H. (1988). *The Superwoman Syndrome*. Adfo Books.

Shapiro, R. (2010). *The Trauma Treatment Handbook: Protocols Across the Spectrum (Norton Professional Books (Hardcover))* (1st ed.). W. W. Norton & Company.

Siegel, D. J. (2010). *Mindsight: The New Science of Personal Transformation* (Reprint ed.). Bantam.

Sleeping Tips & Tricks. (2020, June 1). Sleep Foundation. https://www.sleepfoundation.org/articles/healthy-sleep-tips

Sweeton, J. (2019). *Trauma Treatment Toolbox*. PESI, Incorporated.

Tipping, C. (2010). *Radical Forgiveness: A Revolutionary Five-Stage Process to Heal Relationships, Let Go of Anger and Blame, and Find Peace in Any Situation* (Unabridged ed.). Sounds True.

Trauma Center Trauma Sensitive Yoga (TCTSY). (2018, February 13). Calo Programs. https://caloprograms.com/trauma-center-trauma-sensitive-yoga-tctsy.html

Vanzant, I. (2017). *Forgiveness: 21 Days to Forgive Everyone for Everything* (Reprint ed.). Smiley Books.

Walker, P. (2013). *Complex PTSD: From Surviving to Thriving: A Guide and Map for Recovering from Childhood Trauma* (1st ed). CreateSpace Independent Publishing Platform.

About the Author

Allison Smiley, MS, CHt, is a holistic and spiritual practitioner, teacher, author, and speaker. She is a certified hypnotherapist, Reiki master, and has a master's degree in psychology with a specialization in trauma and crisis intervention. In addition to her 8-Step Trauma Healing Program, Allison teaches Reiki, meditation, and hypnotherapy, offers a Holistic Practitioner Certification Program, and facilitates spiritual retreats for women. She has published and recorded six guided meditations and two e-books on overcoming emotional eating. Allison is passionate about helping people overcome negative patterns and beliefs that have resulted in anxiety, depression, weight and body issues, and feelings of separation and disconnection. She uses a holistic approach (mind-body-spirit connection) to facilitate healing and restore balance, peace, and well-being with her clients. For more info, visit www.allisonsmiley.com.